ACTING
SOLO

ACTING SOLO

ROADMAP TO SUCCESS

BRUCE MILLER

An Imprint of Hal Leonard Corporation
New York

Published in 2010 by Limelight Editions
An Imprint of Hal Leonard Corporation
7777 West Bluemound Road
Milwaukee, WI 53213

Trade Book Division Editorial Offices
19 West 21st Street, New York, NY 10010

Parts of this book first appeared in some form in *Dramatics* magazine and in the journal *Teaching Theatre*.

Grateful acknowledgment is made to J. T. Rogers for permission to use excerpts from his play *White People*.

Permission for lyrics

"Dance: Ten; Looks: Three" and "Nothing" from A Chorus Line. Music by Marvin Hamlisch, lyrics by Edward Kleban © 1975 (Renewed) Edward Kleban and Sony/ATV Music Publishing LLC. All rights for Edward Kleban Controlled by Wren Music Co.

All rights for Sony/ATV Music Publishing LLC administered by Sony/ATV Music Publishing LLC, 8 Music Square West, Nashville, TN 37203

Printed in the United States of America
Book design by Kristina Rolander

Library of Congress Cataloging-in-Publication Data

Miller, Bruce J.
Acting solo : roadmap to success / Bruce Miller.
p. cm.
ISBN 978-0-87910-375-0 (pbk.)
1. Acting--Handbooks, manuals, etc.. I. Title.
PN2061.M455 2010
792.0'28--dc22

2010022669

www.limelighteditions.com

TO ALL OF US WHO ARE WILLING
TO PUT IN THE WORK
NECESSARY FOR MASTERY

CONTENTS

INTRODUCTION

If you've ever seen the now classic comedy *Tootsie,* starring Dustin Hoffman, you know that the movie hits home many times over about the difficulties involved in making a career as an actor. In fact, on the Internet you will find many websites dedicated to quotes about "the actor's life," and all of them have several selections from the movie. In one telling speech, the central character of the film, Michael Dorsey, played by Hoffman, laments the fact that acting is the only art form where the artist cannot practice his craft without having a job. An artist can pick up her brush and paint, a musician can pick up his bow and run it across his violin, a singer can sing, a dancer can dance. But acting is different. Without other actors to talk and react to, an actor cannot fully practice his craft. Although this is true, . you as an actor can, and should, be working on many aspects of your craft—even if you are working alone.

Analysis, for instance, is an essential part of an actor's craft. Yet very little time is spent in acting class learning how to do it. Analysis leads to choices, and choices are an essential component in making a compelling performance. Brilliant choices sometimes come from inspiration alone, but far more often they result because the actor has set the scene appropriately, has thought through the character's situation specifically, and has considered where and how the story is progressing. In addition, different kinds of plays require different kinds of thinking about them, and proper thinking requires a specific kind of understanding. Comedy, for instance, requires a special kind of thought. Laugh lines are painstakingly created by the playwright. How do you make them work? The work of Shakespeare has a particular kind of language that must be delivered effectively. How do you do it? A song has a specific set of problems, in terms of lyrics and music that require, at least for most of us, more thoughtful input than inspiration alone might bring.

Then there are all the grunt aspects of acting that must be done alone. Memorization, for example. Or learning how to take criticism, or finding the courage and persistence to continue living as an actor even when the slings and arrows of outrageous truth or bad luck are striking us down. How does the actor duck, or bob and weave, or take it on the chin and survive? And who teaches us how to do such things? Certainly, for most of us, these kinds of issues are seldom resolved in group activities.

So this book is focused on the things an actor can, and much of the time, *should* do solo. Some of what you will find in this book is good for the actor's brain, and some will be good for the heart and spirit. All of it will help you survive and grow as an actor. Some of it may even help you grow as a human being.

PART 1
ANALYSIS AND HOMEWORK: HERE-AND-NOW THINGS

CHAPTER

ONE

WORKING A MONOLOGUE

BILLY BOB THORNTON HAS BECOME ONE OF MY FAVORITE film actors. Since I first became aware of him in *Slingblade,* a film that he wrote, directed, and starred in, I have become more impressed with his range, truthfulness, and courage as an actor in each film I see him in. The man is a risk taker and a true chameleon. Even in mediocre fare like *Bandits,* his character work is so impressive that it elevates the movie, and his work in films like *A Simple Plan, Monster's Ball,* and *The Man Who Wasn't There* made my jaw drop in admiration. However, in spite of the high esteem I hold for his acting, he may be the last actor on the block that I would want to bring in to speak to my own students. Regardless of how he may dazzle me onscreen, after hearing what he had to say when interviewed for *Inside the Actors Studio,* and watching outtakes from the distasteful but hilarious *Bad Santa,* I'd say Billy Bob is, well, frankly, a bad role model—and not because of his take on Santa, his personal life, or his film choices.

In spite of being a first-rate script writer himself, Thornton apparently doesn't hold much respect for the script (at least the movie script). In his interview with James Lipton, he openly admitted that he doesn't like to be too familiar with the script before he shoots a scene. It takes away from his sense of spontaneity and improvisation. He'd rather use his instincts than what the script provides. The outtakes from *Bad Santa* seem to support this statement. The footage reveals Thornton changing the dialogue from take to take, often with hilarious results. Who, then, could argue with his talent or with his success?

My problem with his approach is that, first of all, it will not work for the stage, and second, it will not help you as an actor who is still learning your craft to master the skills you will need. These skills can be developed only through learning to analyze a script and then learning to make choices based on an understanding of that script. Let's take a look at the first point.

In film, the script is not considered sacrosanct. The writer sells his work for a relatively large chunk of money knowing that the payment received marks the end of her control over that script. Once the film is being made, it is standard operating procedure to change dialogue and story or eliminate pieces of it altogether—if the director and/or actors think the film is being improved by doing so. Once the film is being shot, the director and his producers have total control over what will be done in order to produce a finished product. In theatre, it is the complete opposite. The playwright may not make much money, but her copyright ensures that what goes up on the stage will be what she wrote. No changes to the script can be made without her approval. That means there is no way around what is written on the page—at least in terms of the dialogue. The ultimate production will be intended to serve the script, not undermine it.

Now the second point. Given that most young actors learn their craft through doing theatre and in the theatre the script cannot be violated, it is incumbent on you to learn how to use the script rather than how to ignore it, circumvent it, or change it. But far more importantly, a good script invariably holds the key to your good performance. If you can learn how to mine what is in the script, you will be on your way to creating a good performance every time you begin a new job. If you do not learn this vital skill, yours will be a trail of hit-or-miss work that will not help you to be reliable as an actor or give you the confidence and control of craft essential for good work. The improvisational work that Billy Bob Thornton shoots for is fine for film where you get an infinite number of chances to produce something the director likes, a moment at a time. But in theatre, the lights go down and you're on—only one chance to get each moment right as you move on to the next one—all the way from beginning to end, each moment affecting somehow the next.

The point is, if you can learn to do the work necessary to produce consistently good theatrical performances, then you can easily adapt those skills later and be as in-the- moment improvisational as you or your director requires. But if you don't know how to learn to use the script now, it is unlikely that you'll ever learn it later.

A few years ago, I went back onto the stage after a fourteen-year hiatus. I took on a role in a three-character play called *White People,* in which each character speaks directly to the audience for about thirty-five minutes. Though the three share the stage, they do not interact with each other, only with the audience. The production had a one-week rehearsal period including run-throughs and preview performances. For that reason, I had to work mostly on my own before actual rehearsals began, and in terms of choices I made, what I brought for the first day of rehearsal was pretty close to what I performed a week later. In other words, for the most part, I was self-directed. I had to be able to analyze my part independently of the director and plan out my performance based on my analysis.

How would you fare in such a situation? Do you have the skills to examine a script and to determine your obligations in service of the script and its story? Would you be able to develop and hone your character in such a way that your work would be compelling, yet consistent with what the script and the director are doing? The situation is not as unusual as it might sound. In fact, in today's theatre market, short rehearsal periods are common, and actors are expected to be able to bring in the goods. There may be little time for improvisation, trial and error, and exploration. The question is, can you do it on your own? If you can't, then you might want to consider spending more time now in developing this critical aspect of your craft. It requires being able to read well and actively. It requires that you ask the right questions of the script and of the playwright who wrote that script. If you begin with the premise that everything in a good script is there for a reason, you will have the impetus to hold what you see on the page in the high regard necessary to do your job effectively.

My part in *White People* consisted of seven monologues. In reality, the piece is one long monologue interrupted several times by another character's speech. But the seven pieces, as I learned in my reading, actually fit together perfectly as one long piece. In other words, no time elapses from one piece to the next.

My opening speech follows. Without any further information from me, read it carefully and see what you can learn about the *given circumstances* (the who, what, when, and where of the script). Just use the script and see what you can come up with regarding the story and the character. As you read, underline, highlight, or jot down phrases that give you clues about the given circumstances. When you have accumulated your list, you might want to write out a profile of the person these clues add up to. We'll compare notes after you have read the piece. Read it as many times as you want or need to in order to come up with the goods. Consider yourself a detective on the case.

The finale of Poulenc's "Dialogues of the Carmelites" swells as MARTIN BAHMUELLER, *in an office way up high overlooking the waterfront in downtown St. Louis, is carried away by the music. It is very late Sunday night but* HE *is impeccably dressed; blue shirt still pressed, red tie knotted perfectly.* HE *yells to us over the opera.*

MARTIN: I always turn it up! Right here! It's these nuns right at the end of the show, marching off to get killed for … Who knows! Heads on the block: chop-chop! One after another!

[*The music is reaching the climax.*]

Listen to that! Those voices! You can *feel* those voices right up your spine. Can you feel that? OK! *OK!* Here's where one of them gets whacked! Listen, listen …

[*The blade falls.*] I love that!

Music like this, it's like food. You understand? Shove it in your mouth, suck on it, chew it—It *feeds* you! And the best part—the *best* part is I can't understand a word. Totally clueless! But, you see, it's not like life. You don't have to battle to think clearly, fight to understand. I mean, you've got nuns, you've got an ax: what more do you need? It's just about the music. You listen to this, you escape. Just for a moment, language isn't important. Words, actions—*choices*—don't matter. For me, right now:

[He *cuts the music off.*]

That is magic. That is to be treasured.

Now, if I could get Steven (my eldest) to listen to *this!* He's into all this "new" music. All this hard-core-head-banging … Whatever! Sounds like the music I listened to when I was his age, just a lot worse. Upstairs, door locked, screaming along at the top of his lungs—Who knows! You're fifteen, that's what you do now. Oh! But the way the boy is *dressed!*

[He *is searching for something.*]

Let me show you a—I mean, buzzed head, steel toed boots: you'd think he was in the Gulag, for Christ's sake. He …

[He *stops.*]

Forgive me. This is not the way I work. *Please.* Walls bare, desk clean: no distractions.

[He *continues searching.*]

I should have had this done hours ago but loose ends, cases to turn over—I don't know how long I'm going to be gone, till everything's … run its course. Came in tonight, before the Monday morning crunch. Need to make sure I'm gone before the—Oh!

[He *holds up a framed photo.*]

Well, here's his sister. Unlike her brother she dresses like a human being. Mary Esther's three years younger. It's amazing how much she looks like Barbara. Mary Esther flew back to New York early this morning. Staying with her mother now, just for a while. Till it's all right for her to come home. I call them the "Mayflower Twins": green eyes and that beautiful blond hair that babies are born with and, somehow, the two of them kept. It's the "Blue Blood" in their veins. Barbara can trace her family tree all the way back to Plymouth Rock. I always told her I married her for her genes. Said I needed girl like her if I was gonna get kids from good stock. Mary Esther's smart as her mother, too. Best in her class (Braces now. Hates it. You know the story). I watch her sometimes. Sitting in the car, she's crossing the school yard. She walks with purpose. Twelve years old and she has a sense of life, of its possibilities. You can't teach that. You can only sit back and ...

[He *stops abruptly in mid-sentence.*]

Listen to me! Listen to me, now! This is more boring than talking to my accountant! Even the associates here couldn't feign interest in *this.*

Oh, you should see them! They're in here all day, like a revolving door. Kissing my ass, trying to impress. Two years I've been here and they're still trying to get a handle on the Big Shot from Back East. Figure out how this Brooklyn Boy ticks. Everyone so eager, so chipper. Always bringing me gifts. Bottles of Missouri Wine, Cardinals baseball caps. As if I were some alien from a different planet, never heard of these things.

But what I find interesting—amusing—is their notion of what is acceptable to wear. They're up here in this glass mountain top working for me ten, twelve—What?—sixteen hours a day. Yes, casual is good, casual is nice but this is not their home. We are not here for TV and a barbecue. My first day, I come up here: people wearing loafers, khakis, polo shirts—Things for which they should be shot. I assure you, not anymore.

Now you look at me. You see Egyptian cotton, French cuffs. It says I make money. If you could see my boxer shorts you would know I make a lot of money. This is because I understand The Rules. First off, the suit is cotton or it is wool. Notice the word "poly" did not enter the equation.

[He *gestures to his shirt sleeves.*]

We are not in Kansas, we are not baling hay, these stay down. The knot is tight, *half* Windsor. The shirt is white, starched [blue if you're needing a boost]. No–I repeat–no button down. Button down says I am wearing Fruit of the Loom briefs and they are stained.

This is the uniform! Seal of approval. City of two and a half million people, "Gateway to the West," you think they would know how to dress. You think they would understand the power of conformity.

[HE *gestures to his suit.*]

This is not about looking good. *Please.* It's about That Which Is Reliable. About

The Need for Trust. You're down there, two a.m., raining, cold, who do you run to? Who do you ask the time, for a dollar, for help? You look at me, you know I'm not going to knife you. I'm not going to stomp your face, slit your throat, laugh about it. This is what I tell my associates:

> "The color of your face, doesn't matter. It's the uniform that is safe."

I remember back to my school days in English class, probably eighth grade or so, when we had to read *The Adventures of Sherlock Holmes.* Some of my favorite parts of those stories usually came at the beginning, after the new client had just left. It was then that the great detective would tell Watson all about the individual who had just departed—based on deduction and inference. What Holmes used to do was not that far afield from what an actor must do when he analyzes a script for clues to story and character by trying to determine the given circumstances—based on the evidence at hand in the script. Here follows my list of clues to the story, based on the speech as written above. I have probably missed some things that you have uncovered and vice versa. But let's compare notes. You will see that beside the clues I uncovered, I have jotted down some observations (based on deduction and inference) about what I believe the clues suggest. See how your investigation compares with mine.

(The finale of Poulenc's "Dialogues of the Carmelites")—He likes opera. He may be cultured. But why this opera? Is it consistent with Martin's personality, or did the playwright have something more specific in mind? I'll have to look into this further.

an office way up high overlooking the waterfront in downtown St. Louis—a power office up high with good view. The guy is important or rich.

It is very late Sunday night—weird time to be working.

is impeccably dressed—clothes are important to him. It's late Sunday night, for goodness' sake.

"Heads on the block: chop-chop!"—Sort of a lowbrow response to nuns being executed.

"Here's where one of them gets whacked."—More of the same; surprisingly, he seems more working-class here than cultured, but he certainly doesn't seem to care that we see that in him.

"Music like this, it's like food." The simile suggests that he is in need of something at the moment to sustain him, suggesting that the calming effect of music is at the moment like a basic need. What is his problem?

"You listen to this, you escape. Just for a moment, language isn't important. Words, actions—*choices*—don't matter. For me, right now:"—strongly suggests that he has a big problem at the moment.

[HE *cuts the music off*]—actions as written by the playwright are not random. Why did he cut the music off at this particular spot? Needs to be investigated.

"That is magic."—a moment where words, actions, and choices don't matter is to be treasured and is magic. He must be in a situation at the moment where words, actions, and choices matter greatly, and he needs respite from those things. He is in the midst of a dramatic situation. Not surprising, of course; after all, this is a play, and plays are driven by action. An actor must learn to look for these things.

"He's into all this "new" music. All this hard-core-head-banging

buzzed head, steel toed boots; you'd think he was in the Gulag"—his son is on the neo-Nazi side; the music he listens to is loud and disruptive. This obviously rankles, but Martin seems to be trying to come to terms with it, rationalizing it.

"This is not the way I work"—the implication is that he likes neatness, organization, but his workplace has been disrupted and is out of joint. He has lost control to some degree. The question is why?

"I should have had this done hours ago but loose ends, cases to turn over—I don't know how long I'm going to be gone, till everything's … run its course. Came in tonight, before the Monday morning crunch. Need to make sure I'm gone before the"—he interrupts his thought, or it is interrupted. What causes this? The speech here is filled with clues to the given circumstances. There are no definitive answers, but there are certainly many puzzle pieces. Why is he turning over cases? Why is he leaving? Why does he have no idea how long he will be gone? What must run its course? Why must he be gone before he is seen on Monday morning? It is important to keep in mind that plays, unlike life, are not random. They are organized by the playwright even when they seem random. What connections can be made between the things we know? Can I infer that there is a connection between what has happened to cause his departure, and his son, who has been mentioned several times?

"Oh!"—something has happened in the moment. An "Oh!" is a reaction to something specific. What is it?

"Unlike her brother she dresses like a human being"—seems to imply that Steven is somehow subhuman, and/or certainly is held in less regard than Mary Esther.

"Mary Esther flew back to New York early this morning. Staying with her mother now, just for a while. Till it's all right for her to come home."—the question is why did she fly to New York to stay with her mother temporarily, and how is this connected to Martin's departure from the office?

"Mayflower Twins"—Martin seems to highly value being attached to WASP roots.

"beautiful blond hair"—Martin seems to highly value being attached to WASP roots.

"Blue Blood "—Martin seems to highly value being attached to WASP roots.

"Plymouth Rock"—Martin seems to highly value being attached to WASP roots.

"I always told her I married her for her genes"—Martin seems to highly value being attached to WASP roots. What do these references suggest about Martin? About the play's action? The play's overall idea or themes?

"Best in her class"—Martin seems to take great pride in his daughter's academic standing and success.

"Twelve years old and she has a sense of life, of its possibilities."—suggests that Martin admires the American values of choice and success and wants to see that quality in his children. Esther's approach to life contrasts with son Steven's "anti" phase—his Gulag dress and hostile music.

"Kissing my ass, trying to impress"; "Big Shot from Back East. Figure out how this Brooklyn Boy ticks."—can infer from these references a large ego, an enjoyment of his position of power, and a delight in being the center of attention, especially when he connects his current position to his formative roots. Note how Brooklyn plays against the roots of his wife, the blueblood.

"They're up here in this glass mountain top working for me . . ."—again the image of being on top of the mountain as others below work for him—to infer that he relishes his power is not a big jump.

"My first day, I come up here: people wearing loafers, khakis, polo shirts—Things for which they should be shot. I assure you, not anymore."—suggests that clothes are important to Martin and that appropriate dress is an essential part of doing a particular job well. The manner in which he indicates that his staff now dresses to his taste suggests that he brooks no resistance and has little patience for differing points of view. This is inference, but it is supported by what follows.

"You see Egyptian cotton, French cuffs. It says I make money. If you could see my boxer shorts you would know I make a lot of money. This is because I understand The Rules."—this reinforces the previous note in a specific way. The reference to rules suggests a rigidity about conformity, societal norms, and status.

"This is the uniform! Seal of approval"—again, this reinforces the previous note.

"You think they would understand the power of conformity."—a further reinforcement, but Martin also seems surprised that others don't realize this, or in other words, that others' attitudes could differ from his own.

"This is not about looking good. *Please.* It's about That Which Is Reliable. About The Need for Trust."—is his concern about dress really not about vanity at all? I'm not sure yet. I do not have enough information. Does "reliability" refer to what the clothes tell us? I believe it does, but I will want to find more about this. Does "trust" relate to reliability? I think it does, but I don't know him well enough yet. If this first speech of Martin's were the entire role, I would make choices now. Since that is how we structured the exercise, I will draw conclusions based on inferences that are not quite congealed. But I can make the case based on everything else he has said prior to this. There is vanity, I think, but he also does consider dress to be suggestive of a lawyer's trustability and reliability in the same way the uniform of a policemen would.

"The color of your face, doesn't matter. It's the uniform that is safe."—There is a reference to race here. What is that all about? What does it tell us? I think it tells us, since the playwright put it there, that race is on Martin's mind. After all, what is the name of the play?

All right, now that we have gathered all this information just by examining the words of the script, what have we learned about Martin, his situation, and the rest of the given circumstances of the play? Study your clue sheet and mine and try to make a composite. Put what you have learned into a few paragraphs that, when read, will get to the essence of who Martin is and the situation of the play as you understand it. When you have finished, compare your composite to the one that follows:

Martin Bahmueller is a powerful and high-profile middle-aged lawyer in charge of a large firm with many associate lawyers under him. He is very well-to-do, opinionated, and judgmental. He thinks that he is right about most things and does not brook others' opinions too easily. He is separated from his wife and has two children who live with him. His workplace is located in downtown St. Louis, and his own office stands high above the city and overlooks the Mississippi. Martin is from Brooklyn originally and probably still shows traces of this background in his speech and in his manner. His dress, top of the line, probably is an attempt to compensate for this origin but is also part of the uniform of reliable lawyer that he feels is essential to his success. He likes classical music and opera, but he does not know a great deal about it. He is probably self-taught, and it is something he probably has picked up as an adult. He listens to this kind of music in times of stress and likes it because it provides him an escape from the dominant logic-driven side of himself and allows him to escape his mind, which is always going at high gear.

It is late on a Sunday night, and Martin is packing his belongings after working several hours on cases that he will be turning over to others. He is leaving the firm, at least for the moment, and must be out of the office before work begins on Monday morning. He does not know when he will be returning. His office is a mess, and he hates that fact. Whatever has caused this turn of events has affected his entire life. His twelve-year-old daughter, Mary Esther, an excellent student, is moving temporarily back to New York to live with her mother. His estranged wife, Barbara, is a genuine WASP, a fact that is a source of pride for Martin and is obviously something that he values greatly. His daughter, the image of his wife physically, is a favorite of Martin and, unlike his son, Steven, who is going through a rebellious stage, is on track to have the kind of success Martin most values. On the other hand, Martin is somewhat forgiving of his son and tries to rationalize that he was not so different when he was fifteen, the age of his son.

Martin was hired for this job because he is a "take charge" kind of man. In the couple of years he has been here, he has made great changes in the way the firm conducts business and in the manner that those who work at the firm conduct and present themselves. He is proud of the changes he has made. Nevertheless, there is a bit of resentment in him for the midwestern mentality of those he works with, and he believes that these values will keep the firm from reaching the excellence of the best eastern firms. He certainly believes that you are how you appear.

How does your summary analysis compare to mine? As I reread mine, I got a sense of Martin and an inkling of his situation. I have the beginnings of a profile to build from. But ultimately, it will be my responsibility to tell the story of the play and of my character through what I say and do. If I were to go back and read over the script again, it would be awash in what I have learned about the character and situation through this process we have just gone through. However, we are far from any finish line yet. In spite of having so much more information, I have yet to begin the process of finding the actions of my character, physical and psychological, nor have I begun to determine how I will say the lines that should effectively reveal the story and my character. It is my actions, ultimately, that will reveal character, not my adjectival description. Adjectives provide qualities that cannot be played directly. But actions can. From well-chosen action, an audience can distill quality. But attempting to play a quality will not get the story told.

Thus far, because I have asked you to read Martin's first monologue as though it stood alone, you could not possibly have gotten the complete story from what is there. A playwright structures his work carefully, incrementally, so the onion skin of story unfolds to an audience in the most interesting and compelling way possible. But as an actor you must know the whole story before you can begin to make choices. It is your job to find a way to maximize the conflict, to make the stakes as high as possible, the needs as great as possible. Though you will have to live in the moment and never know more than the character you are playing does at a particular time, your choices must derive from knowing the whole story and maximizing the story at each moment. For that reason, I am going to give you one very important piece of information that is revealed in the play, five speeches later. The news is this: Martin's son Steven has been arrested for committing a brutal hate crime against a young African American couple. Even now he is being held in custody by the police. Reread the monologue with this vital piece of information in mind and see how the speech has changed, intensified, becomes more clear and compelling. How Martin's objective in telling this information is more apparent. Remember, the higher the stakes, the better the story.

With all this new information, go back to the monologue once again and begin to look for the following:

- **Major moments of interest that can be played through physical actions**

  You will need to start thinking of the piece in terms of what the character does—physically as well as what he is going through psychologically and emotionally.

- **The journey that Martin makes during the length of the piece**

  What is he like at the beginning of the piece? By the end? What is the specific route that caused these changes in him? A good story always has a good arc, plot-wise and character-wise. It is your job to find that journey. Try to discover the moment-to-moment route the character travels.

- **Specific islands of import in that journey—places where moments can be made, revealed, and/or portrayed dramatically**

  A found moment gives an actor the opportunity to reveal something specific about his character or the story, and offers him the opportunity to communicate that information to the audience through a well-played action. Can you locate points where the actor as character can reveal the discoveries he is making, the victories he is sharing, the defeats he must deal with?

Jot down any notes as they occur to you. Mark up the monologue as needed. Remember, it is your job to tell the story of this monologue clearly and compellingly. Your journey through the arc of the monologue will be marked by the moments you can clearly make for yourself, but more importantly for the audience. The choices you make for your character must serve to maximize the story being told and to bring out the ideas about the world that the playwright is asking the audience to consider.

FINDING MAJOR MOMENTS

Let's take a closer look now at some examples of the kinds of moments that J. T. Rogers gives us in his *White People.* In Martin's first speech of the play, for instance, he mentions that he has a daughter who:

> … flew back to New York early this morning. She's staying with her mother now, at least for a while, until it's all right to come home.

Since these lines come very early in the character's arc, their importance would be unlikely to land heavily in an audience's minds. The audience would have too much to process as Martin begins to address them. They would be forming first impressions and a general reaction to Martin's looks, the way he speaks, and so on. But the lines themselves do raise issues. Why was Martin's daughter flying back to New York? Why is she staying with her mother now, for a while? Why was it wrong for her to be here now? Why might it be all right later? These are important issues, certainly for Martin and for the audience, but the audience is not likely to be ready at this point to address them.

However, despite the audience's focus, this information about losing a daughter is certainly painful to Martin and a big news item for him. The script makes only a vague reference to this *something* going on—this *something* that is happening within an indeterminate time frame that will be resolved up the road, the how and when unknown. But for Martin, this, too, is obviously a big deal. The lack of detail may let it get by the audience. As an actor, however, I am obligated to play the given circumstances, though the script tells me that I must do so in a way that does not sabotage the playwright's storytelling choice—to withhold information now, for a payoff later.

Martin also tells the audience the following information about packing his office late on a Sunday night:

> I should have done this hours ago, but loose ends, cases to turn over. Don't know how long I'm gonna be gone before all this runs its course. I came in tonight before the Monday morning crunch, got to be gone before the …

Look at all the veiled information the playwright and the character have provided here—that he must turn over his cases to someone else, that he is leaving the firm for an unknown amount of time, and that he has to be gone before he is seen here at the office. This is all major, but since no context has yet been developed and the audience has not yet been hooked into the character or situation, most of the information will slip past them for now. However, these facts are extremely important to Martin—in fact, in his life they are cataclysmic. He is being forced to leave his position. He is packing up his professional life and doesn't know when, if ever, he will again be able to unpack it. In each speech, as the play progresses, more and more plot pieces are laid out on the board, and little by little, pieces here and there start to fit neatly together.

Notice what interrupted Martin in the quote above the preceding paragraph. It is the picture he finds of his daughter or perhaps his wife and daughter together. What impact will seeing the image of his daughter—a daughter who has just left him and returned to New York to be with her mother, his estranged wife—have on him? Martin also shows the audience a picture of his son or, depending on how it is physicalized, at least starts to. What might the impact be of looking at his son's image have on him? Is he looking at a picture of his son as he looks now, or is it a picture from a more innocent, happy, and hopeful time? Which is a better choice? Think in terms of telling the best possible story. How will the choice be demonstrated to the audience?

FINDING THE ARC AND OBJECTIVE

How will Martin relate to and address the listening audience overall? What emotional undercurrents will be his as he reports on the unraveling of his life? How can the actor portray these kinds of victories, defeats, discoveries in the ongoing moments of the play? Keep in mind that it is the actor's job to tell the story of the play and the character through actions – (not simply by revealing emotions)—actions that leads to a whole new level of inquiry.

Why is Martin addressing the audience in the first place? Yes, it is a convention of the playwright to have his character break the fourth wall and address the audience, but, for the actor, there is still the matter of justifying the playwright's choice. In fact, everything a good playwright does in his work is there for a reason. And it is always the actor's job to determine that reason and use the answer effectively. If Martin speaks to the audience, the actor must determine his need for doing so. What is it that Martin is seeking from his audience of listeners? The actor playing Martin must know this. Ultimately, it will give the actor purpose and help him find ways to deliver his lines effectively and compellingly.

Martin is sharing his thoughts and, as a byproduct, his feelings, to a group of intimate strangers. What is his need to do so? The actor playing Martin must come to terms with this question, and he must find his *objective* for doing so. In other words, what does Martin want from the audience? What does he need from them? Once the actor can answer this question, it will give him the foundation for the way he handles his entire relationship with them, the way he addresses them. Once the actor playing Martin has an objective to play, any emotion attached to his purpose can come out as a result of the played actions, rather than as a limiting and undirected be-all and end-all in itself. Though the situation is emotionally fraught for Martin, playing emotions directly will not help the actor build a clear and compelling arc of story in a step-by-step fashion. But playing the need and finding tactics to get what is needed from the audience will.

In the next chapter, we'll take a closer look at the information found in the bullet points listed earlier as we examine another telling monologue by Martin later in J. T. Rogers's play.

CHAPTER TWO

MORE ON MONOLOGUES

IN THE PREVIOUS CHAPTER, WE TOOK A VERY CLOSE LOOK at the first of several monologues spoken by Martin Bahmueller in the play *White People* by J. T. Rogers. Through a careful examination of the words, ideas, and implied or stated actions of the character, we managed to put together a personality profile based on specific pieces of evidence or clues from the text. Here again is what we learned about the character through inference and deduction based entirely on the speech as written:

> Martin Bahmueller is a powerful and high-profile middle-aged lawyer in charge of a large firm with many associate lawyers under him. He is very well-to-do, opinionated, and judgmental. He thinks that he is right about most things and does not brook others' opinions too easily. He is separated from his wife and has two children who live with him. His workplace is located in downtown St. Louis, and his own office stands high above the city and overlooks the Mississippi. Martin is from Brooklyn originally, and he probably still shows traces of this background in his speech and in his manner. His dress, top of the line, is probably an attempt to compensate for this origin but is also part of the uniform of reliable lawyer that he feels is essential to his success. He likes classical music and opera but he does not know a great deal

about them. He is probably self-taught, and it is something he probably has picked up as an adult. He listens to this kind of music in times of stress and likes it because it provides him an escape from the dominant logic-driven side of himself and allows him to escape his mind, which is always going at high gear.

It is late on a Sunday night, and Martin is packing his belongings after working several hours on cases that he will be turning over to others. He is leaving the firm, at least for the moment, and must be out of the office before work begins on Monday morning. He does not know when he will be returning. His office is a mess, and he hates that fact. Whatever has caused this turn of events has affected his entire life. His twelve-year-old daughter, Mary Esther, an excellent student, is moving temporarily back to New York to live with her mother. His estranged wife, Barbara, is a genuine WASP, a fact that is a source of pride for Martin, and is obviously something that he values greatly. His daughter, the image of his wife physically, is a favorite of Martin, and unlike his son, Steven, who is going through a rebellious stage, is on track to have the kind of success Martin most values. On the other hand, Martin is somewhat forgiving of his son and tries to rationalize that he was not so different when he was fifteen, the age of his son.

Martin was hired for this job because he is a take-charge kind of man. In the couple of years he has been here, he has made great changes in the way the firm conducts business and in the manner that those who work at the firm conduct and present themselves. He is proud of the changes he has made. Nevertheless, there is a bit of resentment in him for the midwestern mentality of those he works with, and he believes that these values will keep the firm from reaching the excellence of the best eastern firms. He certainly believes that you are how you appear.

In preparing any role, it is essential that you understand the given circumstances of the play intimately. This understanding includes not only who the character is, as just described, but all of the background information that the playwright provides, through dialogue, set description, direct action, implied action, and so on. That, of course, starts with a careful and detailed reading of the play. Though the word *reading* is singular, for the actor, a thorough reading of the play probably amounts to many readings, so many, in fact, that every detail that the playwright has provided not only becomes clear, but has its purpose in the script revealed to the actor in such a way that he can actively use what he has learned. In other words, you must become so familiar with the script that you can actually translate what you have learned into actions playable onstage. In order to do that, as pointed out in Chapter 1, you will need to look closely for the following:

- **The throughline or arc that your character makes during the length of the piece**

  What is the character like at the beginning of the piece? By the end? What is the specific route that causes the changes that occur in him? A good story always has a good arc, plot-wise and character-wise. The bigger the journey, the better. It is your job to discover the arc. You will also need to map out the moment-to-moment route that your character travels.

- **Specific islands of import in that journey, places where moments can be made, revealed, and/or portrayed dramatically**

  A found moment with a well-played action gives an actor the opportunity to reveal something specific to the audience about the character or the story being told. If you can locate the points where your character can reveal things about himself—his victories, his defeats, his discoveries, and so on—then you're off to a good start.

- **Major moments of interest that can be played through physical actions**

  Once you map out the arc, you will need to start thinking of the arc in terms of what the character does—physically from moment to moment during the course of the play, and as a result of what he is going through psychologically and emotionally. Remember, you can't necessarily show an audience what you are thinking or feeling, but you can execute physical choices that will suggest to an audience what those thoughts and feelings are. It is worth considering from the beginning of your preparation where the big moments for your character are, and how you will convey them to an audience. Naturally, you will not be able to solve all the problems of your performance during your homework phase, but the well-prepared actor starts to think about them right at the get-go.

Remember, it is your job to tell the story of any play clearly and compellingly. Your journey through the arc of any story will be marked by the moments you can clearly make for yourself, and, more importantly, for the audience. The choices you make for your character must serve to maximize the story being told and bring out the ideas about the world that the playwright is asking the audience to consider. The best way to accomplish this is by getting into the habit of first reading your script actively many, many times. Active reading means asking questions along the way. About everything in the script. The playwright puts nothing in her script that is not relevant. If you skim over anything in the map, you will not reach your destination in an efficient manner, if you ever reach it at all. It is your responsibility to learn to analyze all that you have read in a manner that will lead you to great choices—choices that will make your work and that of the playwright the most effective that each can be.

There is another bullet point that must be considered from the very beginning of the analysis process. This is true for any play but has particular importance in a play like *White People,* where the character speaks directly to an audience.

- **What is your objective—in the overall play, and in every scene? What do you need from the characters that share a scene with you?**

  Whatever the answer is, this objective must be played at all times, so it is critical that you are very clear about what this objective is. And in the case of *White People,* you will need to ask what it is you want or need, at all times, from the audience to whom you are speaking. That is, why do you speak to them—beyond the fact that the playwright has mandated you to do so?

  Coming up with an answer to the question about objectives will help you deliver the dialogue with purpose and help you choose the physical actions that will make up your character's presentation. In the case of *White People,* it will also help you shape your dialogue for the audience and will ultimately help you discover and communicate who your character is. The audience, in turn, will be analyzing what you say and how you say it. By the climax of the play, the audience will have formed its opinion of you, and the opinion they hold must be one that will permit the end of the play to work effectively. In other words, the opinion they have formed of your character must be one that brings the play to its proper climax and that allows the play's meaning to be revealed.

In the last chapter we looked at Martin's first speech in the play. What follows here is his third. In the second speech, unprinted in this book, Martin talks about his son's lack of standards, his unkempt manner of dress, and his total disregard for authority and lack of decorum, among other things. If you have not read Chapter 1 recently, you might want to do so now before reading the upcoming monologue, but certainly review the character analysis reiterated at the beginning of this chapter before reading on.

Martin: This is what I'm talking about. This was typed for me late Thursday and on my desk, as instructed, when I came in Friday morning. I'm on the line to Sodom by the Sea (that's L.A.), I'm about to fax it through, first I take a *last look.* One page, three errors. This is unacceptable. My son doesn't get away with this in his book reports! I sit him at the kitchen table, I read through, I mark it up, I say:

"Steven, God is in the specificity. You're smarter than this. You can do better."

This is what I tell Diane, my sec … Executive Assistant:

"Diane, you are smarter than this. You can do better."

Well, she starts in:

"Mr. Bahmueller, I didn't realize …"

What is not to realize?

[*Indicating the letter.*]

This is The Law. This is what tells us what is right and what is wrong and gives life sense. This is to be revered. These words: this is who she is. How can she not understand that? Sometimes they matter, sometimes not? No! You're either lazy or you're not. You can't be both. Half the time it's like—it's like she's a platypus.

"Diane, are you a fish? Or are you a mammal? Make up your mind!"

Oh, she's a fighter. Tongue like a razor. I like that. I just don't like it when she keeps her head up her ass.

She's black, by the way.

I mention this because I would guess you didn't think so. Some of the words I just used they're not allowed when discussing people of certain pigment. Skin color gets in the way of evaluating skill. I am not trying to be ugly, I am making a point. *Now,* you help me here. Here's where it breaks down for me. Caroline, down the hall, when I give her criticism, when I have a problem with her work, that's that. Needless to say we share a similar hue. Now, with *Diane ... Please.* We're not allowed to—We can't just deal with the—the specific *issue* in question. There's always this emotional, this irrational *thing* between us. Twisting. Distorting. *She* feels it, I feel it. But how do we *talk* about it? Friday morning, this letter, we're smiling, huddled over this desk, I'm telling her what's wrong, I'm looking in her eyes and they say:

"You are putting chains on me. You are holding me down."

No, I'm asking you to change a comma. There is a difference.

I don't care if she's brown, mocha, ro-co-ca—Whatever! There are things more important. What you say, how you think: *this* will be your success or your failure. The average person, across the board, our vocabulary is—What?—some two thousand words. You can use them, wield them, dazzle and delight. One slip up and you can kiss your future good-bye. Just one. You take three words—"I," "Doing," "Be"—use them *in* a sentence. "I be doing this." "I be doing that." Might as well have a sign on your back: BURGER FLIPPER FOR LIFE.

> You find me one person—black, white, boysenberry surprise—job like this, making my money says "I be doing." *One person.*
>
> Don't tell me language isn't most important. Don't tell me words don't matter.
>
> [*Another car goes by in a flash of headlights.*]

On the assumption that you have read Martin's third speech several times, let's now examine it using the bullet points listed earlier in this chapter.

JOURNEY OR ARC

Consciously or unconsciously, the good playwright creates a story in which the central characters go on a journey, sometimes literally, sometimes not. But if a character is not somehow different as a result of what she goes through during the course of a play, it is unlikely that the play will be interesting. Generally speaking, the bigger the *journey* or *arc,* the more interesting the play is. This is true for the smaller units of the play, as well. Since, for the purposes of this chapter, we have only Martin's speech to use as an example, let's consider the arc in his monologue about his executive assistant and language. What exactly is the journey that Martin makes during the course of the speech? How is he different at the end than he was at the beginning? Or if he has not really changed, then what has happened during the speech that makes him seem different to the audience? It is up to you as the actor to find this difference and, if possible, mark the journey by using the script as your map. Once the journey is understood, then it is up to you to translate your understanding into actions that can lay out in sequential form the step-by-step arc for the audience. Finding this arc is what will make not only the story, but *you* interesting onstage. And it is your job as storyteller to make what you do compelling and clear—whether the play itself is or not.

At the beginning of the speech, for instance, Martin might be perceived as a person concerned with the sloppiness in values and ethics that has overcome our society. He seems to focus on the way we as a society have come to use language as a reflection of that sloppiness. He attempts to make a case for the fact that sloppiness in language reflects our overall sloppiness in everything we do as a culture. But then he points out that his assistant, the one who has made three errors on one page of an important document, is black. Instantly, we as an audience are galvanized. What does race have to do with this, we want to know? Is this racism, or is there another sociological point being made here? Martin then complicates matters by saying another white employee takes criticism better than his own sensitive-about-race black assistant. Is Martin racist, or is he just pointing out that the race issue muddies up the issue of demanding a high standard in the workplace? We wait for more in order to clarify our confusion. But the mere fact that Martin talks about race in this manner puts our hypersensitive antennae high into the air, and our enculturation makes us lean toward, if not commit to, the conclusion that Martin is prejudiced. Then Martin refers to using black idiom in the workplace—suggesting that it sounds ignorant or, at the least, uneducated, and is therefore what may be holding back members of the black race. He concludes his argument with the assertion that language and its use is the subject—and the means by which blacks hold themselves back.

Many of the points Martin makes here will be applauded by some, reviled by others, but most will agree that there is an element of truth in what Martin says. Where individual audience members stand on these very issues will no doubt influence their opinion on whether Martin is a bigot or not. And that is the very point that J. T. Rogers makes throughout his brilliantly worded play. No matter which side of the aisle you sit on or whether you stand right in the middle of the aisle, the fact is that Martin delivers a series of bombs that continuously shift the audience's perception of him through the course of the monologue. This dynamic will provide the actor playing Martin with an arc, and the actor playing Martin must be aware of this and make choices accordingly.

The fact is that Martin believes what he says to be true and assumes that the audience agrees or, at the least, is willing to listen without resistance. How do we know this? Because there is nothing in the script to suggest otherwise. Martin proceeds as though the audience is offering up no resistance to his point of view. The important thing for the actor is to commit to Martin's beliefs without imposing any of his personal beliefs onto the character. The play must be allowed to do its work. You as Martin must make your case. That is your objective. You will need to play that objective at all times.

DISCOVERING THE MOMENTS AND MAKING THEM

There are many "money moments" in this monologue. Your job is to find those moments and use them well. When you find a money moment, you must discover a way to effectively lift it from the printed page and convert it to a physicalized moment of action in your delivery to the audience. You must do this if you are going to add to what playwright Rogers has already provided. When I say that you must physicalize the moments, I don't mean you must engage in a choreographed series of actions. I simply mean that an audience can know what you think and feel only through what you say and what you do physically. This physicalization includes the things that you actually do, as well as the way you deliver your lines. If you believe, as I do, that the script is only a blueprint for the work an audience will see, then you must find ways to define and add to what the playwright has given you. Otherwise, the audience might as well just read the play and save the price of a ticket.

Reprinted below are several snippets of dialogue that I considered big moments when I was working on and performing the role of Martin in *White People.* You might disagree with some, or you may want to add other items to my collection. I could have suggested additional ones, myself. But, for the purpose of examples, the list here will serve. Read over the selected quotes and see if you can tell why they made my list. Be sure to think through your reasons specifically before you move on to the next one. Also imagine how you might enact each of these moments onstage in order to maximize their effectiveness.

Remember, it is your job to tell the story of the play as well as the story of your character. Your character choices must support the intentions of the playwright's overall story. When you have spent the necessary time on each quote, compare your reasons and methods for execution to the explanations I have listed. There are no single correct answers. There are only choices that work or don't. Your job as actors is to find and execute the best choices you possibly can in order to be believable and tell the best possible story while serving the script.

"One page, three errors."

"'Steven, God is in the specificity. You're smarter than this. You can do better.'"

"This is what I tell Diane, my sec … Executive Assistant:"

"This is The Law. This is what tells us what is right and what is wrong and gives life sense. This is to be revered. These words: this is who she is."

"Oh, she's a fighter. Tongue like a razor. I like that. I just don't like it when she keeps her head up her ass."

"She's black, by the way."

"Some of the words I just used they're not allowed when discussing people of certain pigment."

"Skin color gets in the way of evaluating skill."

"Caroline, down the hall, when I give her criticism, when I have a problem with her work, that's that. Needless to say we share a similar hue."

"There's always this emotional, this irrational *thing* between us. Twisting. Distorting. *She* feels it, I feel it. But how do we *talk* about it?"

"'You are putting chains on me. You are holding me down.'"

"No, I'm asking you to change a comma. There is a difference."

"What you say, how you think: *this* will be your success or your failure."

"You take three words—'I,' 'Doing,' 'Be'—use them in a sentence. 'I be doing this.' 'I be doing that.'"

"Burger Flipper For Life."

"Don't tell me language isn't most important. Don't tell me words don't matter."

All of the snippets above qualify as moments as far as I'm concerned, because each suggests something very important about Martin and furthers the story as well as the meaning of the play. Following this paragraph you will find some brief comments regarding why I think these pieces of dialogue are important, and suggestions on how an actor might build story and character. I have also included some samples of physicalization that I employed at these moments. Please do not interpret that what I chose to do physically constitute the only right answers. They do not. I have offered them up only to demonstrate that physical actions can emphasize and clarify the choices an actor comes up with when analyzing a script.

"One page, three errors."

How infuriated is Martin made by this sloppiness? Your choice will shed light on Martin's character and bring out one of the major themes of the play. The dialogue itself speaks of low standards and expectations in today's society, its failure to educate properly, and Martin's own refusal to give in to this eroding concept of excellence. The question is how important should Martin make the issue. How intense should Martin be here? I chose to be very intense. When I hit this line, I slapped the letter that I had in hand and, depending on the night, thrust out three fingers with emphasis. I wanted Martin to be on a mission primarily about standards, not race. In my mind, Martin's standards do not shift with race, educational level, or gender. My intention was to mask as much as possible any racism he might possess.

"Steven, God is in the specificity. You're smarter than this. You can do better."

The reference to God suggests that Martin is a man of faith. The rest of the quote suggests that Martin believes all of us should not settle for less than our best, despite the fact that society at large no longer holds that point of view. On "smarter than this," my index finger poked at my temple furiously, indicating that my son needed to think. I played the line like I was actually saying this to my son in the moment, teeth gritted as I said it.

So far, Martin has said little that is questionable. He might even be thought admirable in his beliefs.

> This is what I tell Diane, my sec … Executive Assistant:

Martin's first faux pas. In many business operations, women are no longer referred to as secretaries, usually because their jobs have more responsibility than the secretary title suggests. The term *secretary* tends to be thought of as sexist and retro, and it diminishes the importance of the work that an executive assistant might be doing. The fact that Martin catches himself stating the wrong title suggests that he knows it is considered wrong but that some programming inside him is still wired in a retro way. Does his slip suggest he does not believe in the title change, or is it merely a slip of the tongue? Which is the better choice? Why do you think so? I put up my hands in front of me, both as a defensive gesture and as a suggestion of apology, much as an animal might bend in submission to a stronger foe or rival. I smiled to the audience as I did so, as I recall, to let the audience know that my feelings were mixed.

> This is The Law. This is what tells us what is right and what is wrong and gives life sense. This is to be revered. These words: this is who she is.

Is Martin suggesting that it is the law alone that tells us what is right and wrong, or does the statement allow for shades of gray and individual interpretation? Are these words really who Diane is? Martin seems to think so. What does this say about him? About the way he evaluates people's worth? How should Martin share this information with the audience? What should his tone be; his emotional affect? Why? Keep in mind the story you want to tell about Martin and about Rogers's play. Once again I referred to the page, sometimes still in my hand, other times on the table, where I had put it down earlier. The point I was making as Martin was that a person is synonymous with the work he or she puts out.

> Oh, she's a fighter. Tongue like a razor. I like that. I just don't like it when she keeps her head up her ass.

The fighter reference and the admiration for a sharp tongue I played as genuine—to show that Martin indeed does like a fighter. It gives him an opportunity to admire a trait in a person of color. This shows that his admiration can cross racial lines and softens his bigot potential. The "head up her ass" remark is on the crude side, and since Martin, up to this point, has avoided overtly showing his working-class Brooklyn roots, the remark, when delivered, has a lot of power. Suddenly Martin seems far more capable of being unenlightened—about a lot of things. Here the words themselves seemed more than enough. I put on no physical mustard. Invariably the audience hushed here and remained absolutely still through the next bombshell, which follows immediately on its heels.

She's black, by the way.

The placement of this line after the previous is understated perfection in the writing. The credit here goes to the playwright, J. T. Rogers. Simply saying the line without affect had incredible power for the audience every time I said it. The nightly reactions ranged from a hush to audible intakes of air, often followed by whispers and or squirming. The mere mention of race tends to make theatre audiences uncomfortable. This is the intent of the play, and it speaks to the edgy courage of its author, if not to the play's theatrical brilliance. I felt there was nothing I needed to do here beyond delivering the line and waiting for the audience to recover.

> Some of the words I just used they're not allowed when discussing people of certain pigment.
>
> Skin color gets in the way of evaluating skill.
>
> Caroline, down the hall, when I give her criticism, when I have a problem with her work, that's that. Needless to say we share a similar hue.

The three snippets above build on the shock created by the first skin-color reference, and as the actor I knew that I had the audience in my palm through this section. The audience was so uncomfortable with the content of Martin's words that, like the opening salvo, this part of the speech required no extra mustard. As an objective, I focused on making my case to the audience. Since Martin feels that his opinion is fact—fact that a supposedly race-sensitive audience might not feel comfortable hearing—I allowed no discomfort on

Martin's part to show. I played this section as though I was saying the simple truth—a truth that the audience either does or should agree with, a truth that only Martin is brave enough to utter. I found specific people in the audience to make eye contact with, and I held their eyes whenever possible—to show that I had conviction about what I was saying, and to challenge the strength of their own beliefs.

> There's always this emotional, this irrational *thing* between us. Twisting. Distorting. *She* feels it, I feel it. But how do we *talk* about it?

Up to this point, the monologue's arc has been traveling in one direction, toward painting Martin simply as a bigot. Though Martin starts out the monologue seemingly making sense about the fall of standards, his journey toward the line "black by the way" develops in the audience a growing negative picture of him that continues through the previous group of quotes. But this snippet, about the irrational thing between Martin and Diane, catches the audience's attention in a different way. The typical theatre audience, composed primarily of educated, well-to-do white people, is struck by this "emotional, irrational thing" line because they may have had similar feelings at one time or another. Since these feeling are not politically correct, they might be ashamed of such feelings and might, if asked, even deny them. But every night in performance, I could feel a sea change in the way the audience listened to me at this point. Once I felt that, I was able to have Martin share his thoughts more and lecture less. His delivery became more intimate, more compassionate, his gestures slowed down; they became less emphatic. In acting terms, this was a tactic for fulfilling his objective. He was luring the audience into admitting that they have felt the same way.

> "You are putting chains on me. You are holding me down."

Again, I could feel the audience grow less hostile. Many would be leaning in and listening less judgmentally to me at this point. I suspect that it is a feeling of many educated white Americans, though seldom confessed, that some minorities use race as an excuse to avoid taking responsibility for their actions. Martin is willing to say so. Those who may agree with him in the audience now began to change their attitude toward him, though they might never admit to this fact. Because I as the actor felt this, I let Martin feel it, too. Martin began to play to the new power and self-righteousness he feels. I played this section as though I were sharing my story with a sympathetic family member or close friend.

> No, I'm asking you to change a comma. There is a difference.

> What you say, how you think: *this* will be your success or your failure.

In these two snippets, Martin continues to play to those who may share Martin's feelings. In the first he notes that things sometimes mean just what they mean and to take them to a broader sociological level is unfair and even ridiculous. It suggests a reverse racism, in that nothing can be simply about what it is about if race is involved. I had Martin hammer this point vocally, using "there is a difference" as the hammer. I remember extending my arms outward from my sides as though I were preaching to the choir. The next snippet is a theme of Martin's and of the play, though the "how you think" part has ramifications that Martin has not fully considered. Rogers italicizes the "*this,*" and I found that in the case of this playwright, using what he suggests invariably helps the actor and working against the suggestion does not.

> You take three words—"I," "Doing," "Be"—use them in a sentence. "I be doing this." "I be doing that."

> Burger Flipper For Life.

These two snippets were among my favorites to act in the play. The "I be doing" section and the big punch-line payoff "Burger flipper for life" are both outrageously inappropriate and very funny. This section made the audience extremely uncomfortable, stuffed as the lines are with political incorrectness. Nonetheless, it is so funny that members of the audience either gave themselves hernias trying to keep from laughing, or they burst through their attempts to contain themselves, laughed hysterically, and then withdrew quickly in embarrassment. During this section of play the audience became a living, breathing character, and, as the actor, I played these moments in accordance with what I was getting from them.

During a few, more sparsely attended matinees, the audience was more self-conscious and inhibited. Several, in the smaller audiences, managed to contain themselves and did not laugh at all. But a few did. I would hunt those exposed souls down by literally moving toward them from the stage and would direct the build from "I be doing" to "Burger flipper for life" toward them. They became my allies. If the audience as a whole seemed to be trying to distance themselves from me, I simply became more aggressive in my verbal delivery and threw a line or two in their direction—to keep them uncomfortable, trying to make them address their hypocrisy. I say hypocrisy because, in spite of this section's political incorrectness, there is an element to it that even an upper-middle-class, well-educated individual might agree with. Because the speech is so politically incorrect, the discomfort level becomes incredibly high.

I have been somewhat detailed in the preceding section because I wanted to point out that some acting choices cannot be set in advance. There is always the in-the-moment listening and responding that takes acting to the highest level, where spontaneity adds new and magical things to the work. In a play where actors are working with each other and there is a fourth wall, that magic comes from the actors onstage mixing it up with each other, yet feeding off of the energy they feel from the audience. But in a play where the actor directly addresses the audience as a listening character, in-the-moment choices must be found that use that dynamic. Until an audience is present, the actor can only anticipate what the reaction and dynamic might be, with no guarantee that her analysis will be accurate. The best actors, however, can and will adjust to whatever they receive from their partners, onstage or from the house.

> Don't tell me language isn't most important. Don't tell me words don't matter.

The fact is, in spite of its political incorrectness, Martin does make a compelling argument for language, thought, and action. He knows it, too. Therefore, his triumph is palpable. I always felt a silence in the audience at the end of this speech different than in other places during the journey. It was a silence like that after a bomb attack. The contrast with the noise that preceded it intensifies that silence. Martin and I merged here, and I just washed myself in this lack of sound. For me, as for Martin, it was the sound of total submission from the audience. I stood perfectly still, except for the slow scanning eye contact I made with the house. Finally, I would lift my arms from the shoulders out to the sides as if to say, "See what I mean?" My victory complete.

As in every play or scene, every speech an actor makes contains a beginning, middle, and end, and a journey that must be made. Like a cartographer, it is up to you to find this arc and chart out the islands of dramatic possibility. Further, it is your responsibility to mark the journey specifically by finding the stepping stones of progression in the speech. Each of those stepping stones is also filled with dramatic possibilities, as well as its own mini-arc. If you are a good actor, you will find all these elements in the script as part of your preparation and figure out how to handle these moments—with choices that are clear and compelling. When you can do so, you will be assured of the fact that your work will hold up in performance, no matter what your fellow actors and director can or cannot provide. Only then will you be best serving the playwright, the production, and yourself.

CHAPTER THREE

PREPARING TO ACT A SONG

EVERY YEAR I WATCH SCORES OF HOPEFUL HIGH SCHOOL seniors audition for our musical theatre conservatory program. And at least once during each audition cycle, someone sings something from *A Chorus Line.* The most popular two songs seem to be "Nothing" and "Dance: Ten; Looks: Three" (better known as "Tits and Ass"). It may seem strange, but seldom do students using those particular songs make it to my A list. No doubt most of you are familiar with material from *A Chorus Line,* and I suspect many of you have either acted it or, at the least, seen a production or two. For that reason these two songs should be familiar to you and therefore useful in the following discussion.

Why is it, do you think, that the singers using these great numbers seldom knock my socks off—even when they have a solid voices, maybe even great ones? Even when they have the looks necessary to get many of the best singing roles in musical theatre? Even when they have the perfect T's and A's referred to in the song of the same name? In spite of all these show business advantages, most performers using these songs strike out, at least with me. If this seems totally absurd to you, then listen closely, because I'm about to sing a song just for you.

As you probably already know, today's theatre market is distressingly overcrowded. Even for those with looks, talent, and training, finding a paying job is notoriously difficult. Kids with looks who can sing and dance well are no longer necessarily holding a meal ticket to success; they are merely holding the lottery tickets that let you play the game of hope and wait. Casting agents and directors assume you can sing and dance. What they are looking for, what they have more difficulty finding, are good actors—performers who can act while singing and dancing. The kinds of musicals written today, for the most part, require real acting. So do the old chestnuts, for that matter, since they require a particular style and panache not always called for in a contemporary musical. Why, then, should a casting agent settle for less when—as another song from *A Chorus Line* puts it–they "want it all" and can get it, too.

So, back to the question of why those high school seniors fail to impress me with their renditions of "Nothing" and "Dance: Ten; Looks: Three." By now you've guessed that the solid acting component is missing from their work. But how is that possible if they sing their hearts out and put all the emotion they can into their singing? Isn't that what great acting is all about? The answer is "it ain't necessarily so," because, in most cases, these performers are emoting rather than acting the good stuff at the center of the song.

A song, by its very nature, communicates emotion. When you put your attention only on what the audience is already getting, the story contained in the lyric of the song and the given circumstances that generate the need to sing that song are, if not totally lost, left to find their own way to the audience. It is always the actor's responsibility to tell the story going on at every moment of any performance, whether straight acting or singing.

Let's see what all this means in a song like *A Chorus Line*'s "Nothing." Most of the time, the student using this song at an audition will sing her heart out, pouring every ounce of feeling she can conjure. She'll "dig right down to the bottom of her soul," to paraphrase the song lyric. When she has finished, she will likely look at me for approval, her smile stretching across her face with satisfaction.

"Very nice," I'll say. "You really put your heart into that. You've got a very nice voice."

"Thank you," she will return, still beaming.

"I wonder if you can tell me what that song is about?"

But usually she won't be able to. Yes, the student will be able to tell me that it's about a girl who can't feel what she's supposed to in her acting class, and that her acting teacher was mean to her, but it will seldom go further than that. Since there seems to be no other choice, the singer is forced to play the emotion of the song—hurt and anger, the same emotion that the music is already carrying so clearly.

But suppose my singer had responded in the following way:

"This song is about an actor who wants to make those listening to her understand how a bad acting teacher can destroy one's dream of being a great performer. More specifically, she wants those listening to her to know how that acting teacher, by demanding that she feel things she was unable to feel, almost convinced her that she had no talent. But through praying and faith, she finally came to realize that it was her teacher's instruction that was lacking, not her talent, and, with the help of another teacher, she finally blossomed. When she later learns that her first teacher has died, she sadly admits that she felt 'nothing.'"

Now, isn't this story scenario more interesting and specific? It is also more playable—it is something that you can reliably do onstage, whereas emoting is not. An actor who can effectively tell the deeper, more interesting story to those listening to her, and make them understand just what her character felt as she describes each scene of her story narrative, is a student I want. As a great acting teacher of mine once said, "Who cares if you feel! The good actor gets the *audience* to feel." In fact, this song should do just that, if you, as the actor, tell the story in the song.

"Nothing" is a sequential story, and a good one. It even has a surprising plot twist at the end. When telling a story well, you must focus on the listeners, not on your own feelings. The irony here is that most actors, despite the acting lesson at the heart of the song itself, choose to disregard that lesson. They prefer to follow the advice of Mr. Karp, the acting teacher villain of the song, and focus on their own emotion rather than on the more playable action suggested in the lyric. To do so is usually a deadly error in any acting situation. On the other hand, if the actor can make her audience *understand,* by playing her action or objective compellingly, that audience will also *feel*—the goal of every good performer.

A song, then, is no different than a monologue or scene as far as an actor is concerned. Of course, as the performer you must prepare and handle all musical obligations of the song, but that is not the focus of this discussion.

Following is a list of items that as singer/actors you must concern yourself with before delivering any song.

- The given circumstances
- The reason for singing
- The throughline of action
- The Conflict, objectives, and obstacles
- The specific words
- Repetitions of words, phrases, and verses
- The things that are good and bad in the song

GIVEN CIRCUMSTANCES

Acting a song requires the same kind of background thinking that straight acting does—maybe more so. You need to think very specifically about the who, what, when, and where of your song. Here is a list of questions you might want to consider regarding the given circumstances.

- Who is the character you are playing?
- How can you demonstrate what you know about this character through the actions you take or execute while singing the piece?
- Whom, specifically, are you singing to?
- What does your character want from those you are singing to?
- How do the listeners react specifically to each thing they are told?
- If the character is singing to himself, what is he trying to accomplish? What problem is he working through? What are the discoveries he is making as he continues to sing?
- When is this song taking place? Now? Sixty years ago? At night, in the morning? Winter, summer?
- Where does the scene occur? Outside, inside? On a stage, in his bedroom? In Oklahoma, New England, or Victorian London?

A detailed analysis is critical. It will affect every choice that you eventually must make. Ultimately, these choices will amount to the difference between a generalized performance and one that is beautifully specific and moment-to-moment effective.

THE REASON FOR SINGING

Musicals are built on a very unusual convention—the fact that periodically during the unfolding story, a character or characters will suddenly go from speaking to singing. Perhaps I don't travel in the right circles, but, if you're like me, that doesn't happen too often outside of a theatre. Yet when doing a musical, we ask our audiences to believe that is really happening. Because an audience knows the conventions of a musical, they tend to accept this occurrence, but if you make the jump from speaking to singing effectively, the audience is more easily pulled into the moment. The transition from speaking to singing is best made when the emotional content of the situation becomes too great for words alone. This is consistent with the point I made earlier—that music, by its very nature, carries a lot of emotion. It is up to you to make that transition clear; there must be a need to sing, because words alone won't do. So acting the moments that lead into the song become essential. Watch Fred Astaire or Gene Kelly set up a song with their acting. Note how Judy Garland or Julie Andrews prepare for their song by going through some internal thinking or decision-making process before that first note springs forth from them, and how when it does, the audience understands fully their need to sing.

ARC OR THROUGHLINE

Every song you perform must have a throughline of action, or arc—during the piece your character must go on a journey that causes change within her. Otherwise the piece will remain on one level and perhaps will even be boring. Every dramatic situation requires a forward thrust. The character must not be the same at the end of that journey as she was at the beginning. The given circumstances you have already decided on will provide the reason for the journey, and by the end, your character will be in a different place intellectually or emotionally than at the beginning. She will have won something, lost something, or discovered something that will change, or has changed, everything. A problem will have been overcome, resolved, or evolved into something new to deal with. A story song like "Nothing" has such a throughline built in, because it really is a story. Most songs, however, are less direct in their writing. It is therefore up to you to find and communicate that throughline through your own acting choices.

CONFLICT, OBJECTIVES, AND OBSTACLES

The engine of every story is some kind of conflict. The story contains a problem that its central character must solve, resolve, or get around. This is true for a song, as well. A song requires an actor to resolve some conflict by playing out an objective or action by using the lyrics as well as any other tools (such as physical action) available to her. She must decide why she is singing and make choices using the words of the song to fulfill her objective. In the case of "Nothing," Morales, the character singing, has already solved the problem of feeling "nothing," but in the song she is trying to make her audience understand what she went through and what she learned during the story she shares, so her listeners can profit from her experience.

Just about all songs in a musical are sung to another person or persons in the scene, or they are sung to the self. If they are sung to others, those others are listening and reacting. If the character is alone, the song consists of a continuing thought process through which the singer struggles to find an answer to something that is bothering her. It is like a soliloquy in Shakespeare, where the performer has the option to play the song as though her interior thoughts are spoken aloud, or play it by speaking directly to the audience because the character is allowing the audience to share in that thought process. In either case, an internal or external obstacle stands in the way of your character finding a solution to his or her problem. During the course of the song, that obstacle is overcome, or a strategy for overcoming the problem is found. When singing this kind of song, it is up to you to find and carry out the thought process that will lead you to victory, defeat, or discovery. The clues to this arc are in the lyrics, so you must study the words very carefully. You must remember that this thought process is happening as you are singing, so you must make all discoveries and find the new ideas in the moment, as though they are as fresh to you as they are to those in the audience listening. If you can do this, you will be creating the journey mentioned in the last section.

Here is an example of what I mean. Remember the song "Twinkle, Twinkle, Little Star?" Take a moment now and sing it aloud to clear your cobwebs. Read on after you have sung the song. Were you focusing at all on the words and their significance as you sang? Probably not. Now sing it again—sing it as if you have just looked up at the sky and are rediscovering that the universe is a vast and unknowable place. Treat the stars as though each is a beautiful but unsolvable mystery. Talk to them individually as you sing, as though if you speak to each star just right, it might share something with you. Find each new phrase of the song as if it is an idea occurring to you for the first time. Read on when you are finished. Now compare the singing you just did to the first time through. What conclusions can you draw?

Now let's take a look at some of the lyrics of "Dance: Ten; Looks: Three," more commonly known as "Tits and Ass."

OPENING STANZA

DANCE: TEN; LOOKS: THREE.
AND I'M STILL ON UNEMPLOYMENT,
DANCING FOR MY OWN ENJOYMENT.
THAT AIN'T IT, KID. THAT AIN'T IT, KID.

LAST CHORUS

TITS AND ASS.
ORCHESTRA AND BALCONY,
WHAT THEY WANT IS WHAT CHA SEE.
KEEP THE BEST OF YOU.
DO THE REST OF YOU.
PITS OR CLASS.
I HAVE NEVER SEEN IT FAIL.
DEBUTANTE OR CHORUS GIRL OR WIFE.
TITS AND ASS,
YES, TITS AND ASS
HAVE CHANGED ...
MY ...
LIFE ...!

I have to admit that I have been embarrassed by the performance of this song on more than one occasion. Several years ago, a prospective student did this number for me as her audition song in my New York hotel suite, and it made me more than a little bit uncomfortable. I'm no prude, so don't think the subject matter itself is what bothered me. What shook me up was the fact that some young woman, still in high school, no less, was standing in my hotel room shaking her upper and lower at me for no apparent reason—other than that she wanted me to know that she had good uppers and lowers. She sang as though shaking her balcony and orchestra was the sole purpose of the song, and I had no choice but to look toward the spots she was encouraging me to study.

My point is this. The girl performing this piece made no effort to tell a story with the song. There was no apparent point to the song other than showing me her stuff. There was no throughline of action, no progression, no obstacles to face and overcome. I simply watched at close quarters as she repeated three choruses of T's and A's and performed the accompanying physical actions with seemingly no other purpose than to display her physical attributes. Is it any wonder then that I felt totally uncomfortable?

SPECIFIC WORDS

If at this moment you are thinking that my discomfort is my problem because this song is nothing more than an ode to upper and lower body parts, then I invite you to go back and look at the lyrics very closely. Start with the song's actual title. Notice the real title is not "Tits and Ass." The real title is "Dance: Ten; Looks: Three." The actual title implies something very different than the more commonly used name does, and it far better reflects the actual point of the song.

Dance: ten; looks: three, as the character Val tells her fellow auditioners, is what she used to be rated in audition after audition. Sure, she had the talent, she tells them, but not the looks. And then it dawned on her; she worked in a profession where looks do matter—a lot. And since she wanted to be a success, she would do whatever necessary to make success happen. Her solution—plastic surgery!

Like "Nothing," this song is another "I'm sharing what I've learned, so listen good" song. But in this one, the singer, Val, is less concerned with telling her story than with making her listeners get the point. In a nutshell, the throughline goes from "this is what I used to think and it didn't work," to "this is what I finally figured out," to "and this is what I did about it and see it worked for me," to "it'll work for you, too." If you analyze the first stanza for what it is really saying, and then compare it to the finale of the song, you will see clearly how the song's throughline is specifically delineated.

A careful examination of the given circumstances and the words of the song will also reveal that there is a strong conflict here—one that leads to a strong objective to play and obstacles to overcome. Trying to convince a group of young, still idealistic actors that success in theatre means fixing how you look is not necessarily an easy sell. The actor playing Val must overcome her listeners' innate tendency to believe that talent alone will prevail. Then she must convince them that altering their looks to the better will not change them inside, but will certainly help them succeed in the business. That in turn will make them feel good all over. All of this is communicated tersely in the following lines:

WHAT THEY WANT IS WHAT CHA SEE.
KEEP THE BEST OF YOU.
DO THE REST OF YOU.

Note that these concluding lines are a far cry from the opening lines repeated below:

DANCE: TEN; LOOKS: THREE.
AND I'M STILL ON UNEMPLOYMENT,
DANCING FOR MY OWN ENJOYMENT.
THAT AIN'T IT, KID. THAT AIN'T IT, KID.

Songs, like other forms of poetic writing, tend to cut right to the heart of things. They talk directly about thoughts and feelings, and they sometimes use figurative and elevated language to make their point quickly and efficiently. The actor singing must note this kind of language and use it actively to make the points contained in those lyrics. "Orchestra" and "balcony," for instance, are not generalized locations in a theatre. Tickets in the orchestra are considered better seats (and they cost more) than seats in the balcony. A balcony seat is nice, but people would rather be located in the orchestra. What does all this have to do with body parts? There is a connection that can make for a knowing joke, if played right by the singer performing the song. An actor singing about "orchestra and balcony" must find a way to include as much of that suggested meaning as possible. Examine the beginning lyrics of this song for other examples of specific word selection by the lyricists that communicate far more than a cursory reading might suggest.

Song lyrics tend to be structured in the form of verse and repeated choruses. This means that you will have to say certain things several times over. If you are to keep the story of your song moving forward, each time you repeat a set of lyrics, you will have to not only come up with the reason they are being repeated, you will also have to make them different each time you say them. The difference will probably be suggested by the verse lyrics that come before, but even if they are not, it will be your job to maintain the forward thrust of your storytelling. My young auditioner had many opportunities to repeat "T's" and "A's" when singing to me, but they all pretty much ended up being the same generalized cheesecake, rather than a new take on what her new body parts were starting to do for her, as suggested by the song. Remember, you must use the words of the song to take the audience on a journey. A good throughline will go a long way toward making your piece work.

THE THINGS THAT ARE GOOD AND BAD

A good actor always tries to show as many levels of character and story as possible. This keeps her and the story she is sharing interesting. The music of the song being sung often lulls the actor performing it into a generalized or one-level interpretation. An easy and effective way of keeping yourself from falling into that trap is to ask, "What does the character think is good in the song, and what does she think is bad?" By recognizing and making the distinction between the two, you can quickly add many colors to the song that were not apparent before the exercise was done. Finding what's good and what's bad also sets up many interesting contrasts in the song.

Take a moment and go back to the lyrics of "Dance: Ten; Looks: Three" and read them aloud. When you have finished, decide which things are good and which are bad. You might want to put a little "g" above the good things, and a little "b" over the bad. Whether you choose to write or not, make sure you are very specific as you go through the text of the song. Once you have completed the process, reread the lyrics aloud. There was probably a lot more nuance this time through. What you have just learned can be applied to any song lyric you face for the first time.

CONCLUDING NOTES

The most important point contained in this chapter is the fact that as an actor singing a song, you must avoid playing the emotion the song suggests. Instead, you must find the reason for singing and then make choices that will get you what you need, whether it's finding a solution to a problem or convincing someone else to do something they should be doing. The words to a song are every bit as important as the music they sail on, and it is your job to make those words come alive by using them to tell the story the song contains. If you do the preparation work properly, when the time comes to work on the performing part of the song, you will be well armed for turning that song into the knockout number you want it to be.

CHAPTER FOUR

PUTTING THE SONG ACROSS

IF IT IS NOT ALREADY THE CASE, IMAGINE FOR A MOMENT that you have completed your education and you have moved to New York to begin your career as an actor/singer. For months you have been spending your time auditioning by day and working your restaurant shifts by night. Each new audition you go to takes on increasing importance, because lately you're beginning to think of yourself more as a food server than a performer. You need a theatre job—bad! You've got looks, a great body, and a terrific voice. So how come you haven't landed that breakthrough part yet?

One reason may be that everyone else auditioning for the roles you are auditioning for can say the same thing. There are hundreds if not thousands of fabulous voices for every singing role to be won. So how can you defy the odds and get that role? The answer, of course, is acting. As discussed in the previous chapter, it is simply not enough to have a fabulous voice in today's musical theatre world. You must be able to act, as well. If you read any Sondheim lyric, you quickly realize that the words, the situation, the song's throughline, and the dramatic conflict unfolding are no less important to putting the song across than the music is. If you rely simply on your vocal instrument, you will be falling far short in the musical theatre world of today.

In the last chapter, we talked about the preparation necessary if you are going to be able to put a song across to an audience and sell yourself to the producers and directors casting a show. Here is a quick review of some things you need to think about in order to make those effective acting choices that will help you put your song over.

- The given circumstances—the who, what, when, and where of the situation, either from the script or decided upon by you in order to sell the song
- The reason for singing—your motivation for breaking into song
- The throughline of action—where your character is, objectively and emotionally, at the beginning of the song, and how the lyrics help your character make a journey that progresses dramatically until your song ends
- The conflict, objectives, and obstacles—what are the problems addressed in the lyric of your song, and what do you as your character do to overcome them during the song?
- The specific words—what do the lyrics specifically mean, what do they mean to you as the character singing, and which words help you get that meaning across the most specifically?
- Repetitions of words, phrases, and verses—how you keep these repetitions dramatically propelling the story forward
- The things that are good and bad in the song—the words and images that strike you as your character as good or bad (breaking the lyric down in this manner will help you color your phrasing and give levels to your performance)

A well-performed song not only sounds great, but seamlessly incorporates the results of this kind of investigation to produce a well-acted, dramatically effective song presentation—one that not only demonstrates that you are a fine singer, but a fine actor telling an intriguing story. Let's assume that you have taken care of all the actor homework described here. Now let's go through the steps of your potential performance by examining what you need to do at every step.

SELECTING MATERIAL

The first step in any good performance, whether sung or spoken, is in the selection of material. Pick good material and it can help make you look better than you are. Pick bad material for an audition and even Bernadette Peters might have trouble landing the role. Good song material will stand on its own, even out of context. It will sit well in your voice range. It will offer you a dramatic throughline to play, one that will allow you to progress moment to moment through the story of the song. It will contain a problem to work through, or an obstacle to overcome, or, at the least, it will lead to some kind of discovery that will somehow change you. Good song material will provide you with something to go after or reach for while you are performing the piece. A song in which you find yourself playing a single emotion rather than an action is to be avoided. More often than not, the music of any particular song provides a clear emotional framework for both the actor and the audience. If the lyric does no more than reflect what is already apparent in the music, you're probably making a mistake in using that material.

Just to be sure that you've got the concept, check out the following short quiz:

> Which of the two songs listed below do you think would make a better audition piece?
>
> A. "Row, Row, Row Your Boat"
> B. "Twinkle, Twinkle Little Star"

Obviously, both of these songs fall far short of the ideal audition song, but given the criteria listed above, the answer is definitely B. At least "Twinkle, Twinkle" offers the possibility of some dramatic conflict. It has a potential throughline and a dramatic progression, and it offers up a series of in-the-moment playable discoveries. "Row, Row, Row Your Boat" does not. Which one would you opt for? Try singing through both after providing yourself with some basic given circumstances. Which is more actable? Which gives you more to show at an audition?

DEALING WITH YOUR ACCOMPANIST

The second step in guaranteeing yourself a good singing audition concerns the relationship you establish with your performing partner—the accompanist.

It is your job to keep your partner happy. The power to save or destroy you lies in his or her hands. It is critically important that your accompanist knows exactly what you are planning to do and how you plan to do it. You can't expect that with only a shared word or two that your musical needs will be met. The more you have written on your music clearly and simply, the better your chances for success.

Your accompanist will be happy if you keep his or her life easy and manageable. Your music should be in a binder that is easy to turn, or the loose pages of your song should be taped together in such a way that your accompanist can spread the music across the piano stand easily. Do not expect your accompanist to be able to transpose your song. If you want a particular thing to be played, it should read that way on the page. Any tempo changes or other musical variations should be marked clearly on the score and pointed out if possible. It is your responsibility to discuss with your accompanist when to begin playing and the exact manner in which you will indicate to begin. Keep in mind that when you bring in material that is little known or extremely complicated, you run the risk of being tripped up. You may be angry and blame your accompanist, but the smart professional will always be prepared for all possibilities. If you give away or share the control of your success, you must take responsibility for what happens. Many professionals bring their own accompanist to an audition for just that reason. I am not suggesting that this is what you should do. I am merely pointing out how important it is for you make yourself and your material clear to your accompanist.

YOUR OPENING

Keep in mind that your audition really starts the moment your name is called. You are creating an impression of yourself from the moment your announced name is connected with the body moving across the floor toward the piano. Even before you begin to perform, people are making judgments about who you are and how you might be to work with. Make sure the impressions you create are positive ones. They can help you get or lose a job. The aura you create as you move across the floor, as you discuss your piece with your accompanist, and as you move into position for the performance can sometimes spell the difference between a callback and oblivion.

All right. You've talked with your accompanist, and he or she is now clear about what your musical needs are. You move to your opening position onstage and signal the pianist to begin, perhaps with the agreed-upon nod of your head in his or her direction. The intro music begins, you wait for your cue, and when it is time, you open your mouth and sing. Beautifully.

Hey! Wait a second! Cut! Stop the orchestra! What is wrong with this picture?

The answer is critical. What I have just described above may be an acceptable beginning if you're simply singing a song, but it is not enough if you're supposed to be acting it. Remember, your work as an actor must begin long before you sing that first note. When that musical intro begins, the acting meter is already running. If you wait until it's time to sing before you start acting the story you are telling, you'll probably end up having to chase your cab down the street. Granted, it is a primary convention of musical theatre that characters who are speaking at one moment will suddenly burst into song the next; and as an audience, we will accept this strange behavior. But we will only do so when the transition is well done. When the audience clearly sees that simple words are no longer enough to contain the feelings and ideas a character needs to express, the transition from speaking onstage to singing has been well executed.

In an audition situation, it is your job to demonstrate this transitional moment strongly, specifically, and clearly. Since at a singing audition this transition occurs at the very beginning of the song, and usually without the benefit of spoken words before you actually begin to sing, those opening bars of the song must be well used. Your acting during those bars must demonstrate the thought process that is leading you to sing, and you have only those introductory bars to build up your transitional head of steam.

Here is a basic illustration of what I'm talking about. Since "Twinkle, Twinkle" is universally known, I'll use it again as an example, even though it should never see daylight—or moonlight—at an actual casting call. All right. Imagine that you have taken your opening position at an audition and have signaled your accompanist to begin. As those opening bars are playing, you shift your focus upward toward the heavens, a spot angled above and behind the audience. You scan the cosmos intently, futilely trying to find its terminating point. This, of course, is impossible, you discover, and the awe of what you see above you drives you to sing the opening lyric.

TWINKLE, TWINKLE LITTLE STAR.
HOW I WONDER WHAT YOU ARE.

Despite the fact that you have used this simplistic nursery rhyme song, you have just managed to make the transition from nonsinging to singing in a clear and believable manner. You have also managed an opening moment that has been not only sung, but well acted, too. There you are, two lines into the lyric and staring up toward the ceiling of your audition space. What do you do now? Which brings me to the next topic of discussion.

YOUR FOCUS

Many songs, especially ballads, are at least in part about a character describing a new feeling or discovery, reflecting on past events, or lamenting a problem or failure, usually associated with love. Often these lyrics are interior monologues spoken aloud through song while this character is alone. At other times, the lyrics are addressed to a listening party supposedly present with the singer, and the actor must imagine that presence. Each of these situations requires its own specialized acting responses.

When performing a song at an audition, you basically have three choices in selecting a focus. You can target that imaginary listener, you can acknowledge the audience's presence and sing directing to them, or you can sing your inner thoughts aloud and physically target nothing specific.

If you choose to focus on only one listener as you sing, you can target a single spot behind the audience. Make sure that the listener is very specific for you, and your reason for singing to your listener is very important. It will help you color your choices. Don't worry if these out-of-context choices are inconsistent with the given circumstances of the play from which it came. A singing audition should be able to stand independently and work. Just make sure that your focus remains consistent throughout the song, or the illusion of the listening character will be lost. Also be sure to respond to what that imaginary presence is putting out. In other words, know when and how that listener would be responding if he/she were actually there. You in turn must react as though you are responding to the input your imaginary scene partner is providing.

If you are singing a lyric that implies you are alone, busily reflecting, lamenting, or feeling, there is always the danger of falling into a trap. When your focus is primarily on the emotional aspects of these rather passive actions, the resulting acting choices often end up one-level and ultimately boring. You cannot play sad, happy, or confused effectively, at least not for a sustained amount of time. There is no dramatic progression in that. To avoid this trap, you must always try to make your feelings a part of the given circumstances and then give yourself a strong action to play or need to pursue. Try to find an answer to your problems, make discoveries along the way, and resolve the issues that are troubling you. In others words, have an objective when you are saying your thoughts aloud.

Most importantly, don't play sad or lost. Don't play that you're a loser. Play trying to find the way to win. Your job is not to demonstrate that your character feels. Your job is to make the audience feel. Audiences identify with fighters, those who don't give up. They root for you when you attempt to overcome the odds. They appreciate the effort even if you fail in the end. They do not identify with losers. So don't play one.

It is often easier and more dramatically effective when you address the whole audience for your audition—even if this is not totally consistent with the actual circumstances of the play. You can actively use your audience to bounce off the ideas and the discoveries you are making in the moment. Active use of an audience can also help you keep your objective stakes high, because you must make the listening audience buy into what you are saying. If, rather than simply singing to yourself, you use the audience to share with, convince, or get sympathy from, it is very likely you will be dramatically enhancing your choices. Just be sure not to linger too long on any one member of the audience. You do not want to make anyone uncomfortable by doing so.

Take the song "My Favorite Things" from *The Sound of Music,* for instance. This is a list song—a song in which a lot of images are fired off one after another, and one that might on first glance seem totally without any dramatic progression. Try singing it aloud to yourself. Even if you divide all the images up into good things and bad things, basically it probably came off as a two-level song—things that make me feel good, and things that make me feel bad. But if you target the audience and actually focus on them and use them while singing, "things" will change quickly. Once you have that audience target, the song starts to be about convincing that target listener—the audience—that using favorite things to make you feel better when things are bad really works. That approach to the song quickly turns it from an I'm-feeling-bad song to one that has a conflict, obstacle, and dramatic progression. The lesson, then, is to use the audience whenever possible. Singing to yourself, like acting a monologue to and for yourself, is just plain harder. It has many traps and pitfalls.

But even in a song where you are convinced that it must be sung to and for yourself alone, there are ways to keep the piece from becoming one-level and simply about an emotion. Remember that a good lyric has a throughline. You will move through a series of thoughts and feelings that lead to a conclusion far removed from where you were when you began singing. Your objective must be to find an answer to the problem presented at the top of your lyric. If you weigh and evaluate each new idea, it will take you to the next idea and feeling, which, in turn, must also be weighed and evaluated until you reach the conclusion of the song, usually at its climax.

This journey of ideas, thoughts, and feelings can be conveyed to the audience by physicalizing the discoveries you make along the way. A physical shift, a turn, or a new focus when each new lightbulb goes off for you can make clear the steps of your journey. In turn, these physical choices are likely to make your performance more interesting—since physical choices are active rather than passive.

Try the following physicalization exercise for yourself:

Sing the Alphabet Song aloud. Before you do so, however, arbitrarily divide the song into sections—say, in accordance with the rhythm of the song: ABCD, EFG, HIJK, LMNOP ... et cetera. Physically turn and target a new focus after saying each grouping and see what happens. In all likelihood, you will find out that this physicalization actually helps you create and define transitional moments, and certainly helps make your moments of discovery clearer. Ultimately, this physicalization will allow an audience to see you making your discoveries clearly and specifically. This, of course, is just what you want. By the way, you have just begun blocking your presentation.

BLOCKING—MOVEMENT AND GESTURE

Blocking, or your chosen physicalization onstage, consists of actual movement from place to place, gestures that help you make clear what you are thinking and feeling, and business—any ongoing activity you engage in onstage. In a singing audition, unless your song specifically calls for it, it is better to avoid ongoing business. It will unnecessarily complicate what you are doing and probably take away from your dramatic impact and connection with your audience. But the movement and gestures you create for your song can help enormously with the song's overall effectiveness.

How much or how little blocking you put into your piece is often a subject of heated debate, but a good rule of thumb is that if the movement or particular gesture does not enhance the song, don't put it in. I have heard acting and singing teachers tell students that a particular song is so rich in emotion, so strong in its own narrative, that all an actor/singer need do is stand there and sing it. I have also heard teachers say that gestures simply distract from the inherent beauty of a song, so don't use them. On the other hand, I have seen directors and coaches choreograph so many gestures and movements into a song that it seems more like a game of charades than an acted song. So what should you be doing?

Recently, I had occasion to watch a number of auditions where the performers found their places onstage and literally sang the song in total stillness with arms at their sides, never once moving. In some cases the songs being sung were heartfelt and passionate. But many of these performers struck me as dead from the neck down. How, on one hand, can we say that according to theatrical convention, characters begin to sing because words alone are no longer enough to hold their thoughts and feelings, and then on the other hand direct these characters to remain totally still? My response is that we can't. Don't get me wrong, stillness can be dramatically effective and very powerful. A ballad, for instance, tends to require less movement because the built-in sentiment is so strong. And if your lyrics are dense or complicated and hard for an audience to follow, you won't want to complicate matters by adding unhelpful movement that can end up being distracting. But, more often than not, when it feels right to move, or the impulse to do so is strong, you'd be well advised to at least try what your body is telling you to do.

When moving seems appropriate, try this rule of thumb. Characters move toward someone or something when they need to badly enough. They move away from someone or something when distance is helpful. If your objective is to make someone understand your feelings, chances are you will move toward them, especially if your stakes are high (and they should always be as high as you can possibly make them). If your song is about the need to break up with someone, chances are your movements will be away from your target. Distance protects you. Your job is to find the places in the song where movement would and should occur—places where movement will enhance your work dramatically.

If you decide that there should be several moves heading toward downstage, make sure your opening position is upstage so that you will be moving toward your target beyond the audience without running out of room. If your song is about finding the strength to leave, start downstage and make sure your pull is away from your target toward upstage. Be sure to find those moment where putting an additional step between you and your focal point is dramatically effective. You get the idea.

All right, now let's talk about gestures for a moment. Nothing looks worse or more amateurish than a choreographed set of gestures coming one after another and that seem imposed rather than organic. Gestures are effective only when they seem to believably rise from the feelings created in the moment. They simply must seem natural. Some young actors, for just this reason, avoid gesturing altogether because it feels unnatural to do so. Even at the climax of their song, their arms remain lifelessly at their sides. Ironically, at this point in a song, seeing someone singing so passionately with weighted-down arms looks just as unnatural to an audience as a new gesture might feel to a performer, and it works against the vocal passion being presented from the neck up. Gestures are no different than other forms of blocking. When a director says move from here to there on this line, it usually feels weird—at first. But with repetition, those blocking choices become real and second nature to the actor. It is no different with gestures.

You must be willing to experiment in your rehearsal process. Allow yourself to physicalize or even over-physicalize what you do as you sing through the song. Observe and record what feels most right and what gestures help you make dramatically effective moments—moments that work for you and moments that will ultimately work for an audience. You may not be able to make these judgments entirely on your own with absolute certainty, so of course you should check in with your teacher or someone else whose judgment you trust. But you must be willing to build a vocabulary of physical choices that support the material you are working on. Don't forget that strong emotion produces physical responses, or gestures, in human beings; and, on the other hand, the selection of appropriate gestures often produces corresponding emotions that can help you as an actor. This reflexive relationship makes the gesture an extremely useful tool. The important thing to ask, ultimately, is if you were to remove a gesture you decided upon, would it be missed? If the answer is yes, keep it. Otherwise, don't. There can be no doubt, however, that your physical presentation should be as alive and as vibrant as your singing.

PHRASING AND THE UNSPOKEN

The best singers did not earn their reputations simply because of the quality of their voices, and in musical theatre it is possible to have a career even if you don't sing well, or barely sing at all. Rex Harrison gives one of the finest musical theatre performances of all time in *My Fair Lady,* yet he seldom so much as sustained a note. There are better voices than Frank Sinatra's, but probably no better singers. How is this possible, you ask? The answer is phrasing.

The greatest singers in every genre, from any point in the history of singing—from Tony Bennett, to Elvis, to Andrea Bocelli; from Ethel Merman, to Mary Martin, to Julie Andrews; from Maria Callas to Cecilia Bartoli—all share the ability to use their lyrics as effectively as they use the music those lyrics fly with. If you really want to put your song across, you must begin to think about the following:

- How to select the words you emphasize or sustain
- Where you should breathe to be most dramatically effective
- Where to, and where not to, take a pause and breathe

There are obviously many more considerations having to do with shaping the words for dramatic effect, and these will become apparent as your sophistication about these matters grows with training and experience. However, there are no simple rules of thumb here. Learning to phrase well is a combination of instinct, trial and error, careful study, a knowledge of what works best for you, and practice, practice, practice. The best singer/actors never stop thinking about their phrasing, never stop making new discoveries about the songs they have sung their entire careers.

There are often places in a song where you do not sing, yet the music of your song continues. It is up to you to stay with the song, even if you are not actually singing. Waiting is not a dramatically effective choice. If the lyric of your song stops, it is up to you to supply the subtext so that when it is time to start singing again, you are right there with the music. The dramatic progression must continue, and the audience must understand the reason you have stopped singing aloud, what you are thinking during your pause from singing, and why you begin singing again when you do. Never consider a bridge or an interlude in the music as a nasty little obligation to get past. Instead, consider it as an opportunity for you to do some of your best acting—the unspoken kind. Nothing is more dramatically effective than the filled pause. No situation offers a better solo opportunity than the sustained silence. Begin learning how to use these built-in opportunities now. They can and will get you work.

CONCLUSIONS

Hopefully, you are now better aware that singing is not something you do in a musical during the moments you are not acting. Your obligation to any song requires you to pay careful attention to its acting, as well as its musical requirements. Music and lyrics must go hand in hand—always. The same responsibilities you have to the script when you are not singing apply when you are. The best musical theatre performers are fine actors—with or without the Sondheim score playing behind them.

Even though this chapter has focused primarily on your acting responsibilities in performing a song, it was not intended to imply that your technical singing responsibilities are less important. They are not. You must meet the obligations of a song musically at all times. And for many actor/singers, this means mastering the musical aspects of a song before setting out to work on the acting aspects. It is true that if you are worrying about the mechanics of your singing while you are trying to act, you can become totally frustrated. So you may want to get down the technical elements first. It is also true, on the other hand, that your commitment to the acting of a song can refocus you away from your body mechanics enough so that your learned singing technique has an opportunity to relax into what it knows how to do.

I have often worked with opera singers who, once focused outside of themselves, hit the high notes with an ease and efficiency unavailable to them when they are focused on their technique. It is up to you to find out how your own acting/singing apparatus works most efficiently for you while preparing a song. But whether you start with the chicken or the egg is less important than the omelet you eventually put out there for the audience. In a musical theatre performance your acting and singing must be whisked together so completely that one is no longer separated from the other. If you achieve that blend, your performance should be nothing short of delicious.

CHAPTER FIVE

ACTING IN COMEDY

I HAD BEEN THINKING ABOUT WRITING ON HOW TO PLAY comedy for some time, but after watching four solid actors from my professional acting class struggling with their work—scenes in which I would have thought the basic comedic dynamics were self-evident—I decided to start writing. What I learned from watching those scenes is this: comedy has certain principles that must be observed by actors and directors, but even working professionals can be unaware of these principles. If that is the case, then those principles are probably worth sharing with you now. The truth is that when the basic principles of comedy are observed, people will laugh (if the material itself is funny), but when these principles are not followed, even the most foolproof material can be killed. An awareness of the principles that make comedy go can spell the difference between acting success and failure. So that is the subject of this chapter.

Before we begin, a few introductory thoughts about acting in comedy might be appropriate. Let me start with a question: How often have you heard professional actors say on television or in newspaper interviews that they are dramatic actors and don't do comedy? Or can't do comedy? I know my beginning students say it all the time. Maybe you say it, too. The fact is that the same basic acting principles that apply to drama apply to comedy, as well, but in comedy there is an obligation to make the audience find the work funny. That is the only big difference. Superb actors like the late Walter

Matthau or, more recently, Vince Vaughn began their film careers as dramatic actors before turning to comedy. In fact, Matthau spent years in Hollywood playing psychotic heavies. His best friend, the late, great Jack Lemmon, jumped back and forth effortlessly from comedy to drama throughout his long and distinguished career. And Vince Vaughn played the psychopathic serial killer in Gus Van Zant's remake of the Hitchcock classic *Psycho* before becoming one of Hollywood's best comic actors.

Actors who say they can't do comedy because they are not funny are probably short-changing themselves. An actor doesn't need to be funny any more than he needs to be sad, or angry, or any other emotional quality while playing a scene. What an actor needs to do is play actions—actions that are tangible and therefore doable. If an actor plays a set of tangible actions clearly and fully, the audience gets the feelings behind the actions. It is no different with comedy. If the actor plays the proper actions fully, the script will do the rest. A good comedic script provides the mechanism for getting the laughs, irrespective of how funny an actor thinks he is—if that actor is willing and able to commit to and execute the acting requirements. An actor would not say, "I can't do that role because I don't do sad." Why, then, should he say, "I don't do funny"?

There are, however, certain essential items that an actor must think about when playing in comedy. A failure to do so could lead to the worst possible outcome when performing—silence from the audience. Here is a list of items that an actor must consider when attempting a comedic scene:

- The play's genre and style
- The play's language and how it works
- How to convert the author's wit to the character's wit
- How to recognize and use the conflict as fully or more fully than in a dramatic work, and how to turn that knowledge into strong, playable objectives
- How to listen in the moment, especially to lines that come from a setup in the previous line
- How to physicalize the action in ways that are organic to the scene and to the comic obligation of the character
- How to make choices that serve the story and the character without compromising what is funny in the script provided

You will notice that there is nothing radically different listed here than what an actor might be expected to know in any other kind of scene. There is just a particular focus on the elements that are certain to bring out what is funny in the work. Now let's take a look at how these principles apply to some of the scenes from the acting class I mentioned before, and how the use of those principles might have enabled those actors to avoid the pitfalls they fell into their first time up.

The first scene that I will discuss came from *Four Dogs and a Bone* by John Patrick Shanley, the second from *Private Lives* by Noël Coward—two plays that couldn't be more different in style yet, surprisingly, hold similar pitfalls for the actor who is not accustomed to thinking in terms of how comedy works. Principle number one, then: it is incumbent on you to know the kind of comedy you are performing in and to be able to draw from the rules that apply to that particular brand. The two scenes in question will provide examples of what I'm talking about.

Before presenting their scene from *Four Dogs and a Bone,* the actors working on it explained that they selected it because it was about show business, a subject that both could relate to. The scene itself concerns two actresses who are willing to do anything to get ahead in the business, one younger and getting her first big career break, the other a seasoned veteran trying desperately to hang on to a career that is beginning to fade with her youth. Both characters are working together on the same film, and each sees the other as a threat to her continued success. Each will do whatever she has to in order to succeed. Each will do to the other whatever necessary to maintain her personal advantage. For the casting of the scene, the younger of the two actors played the older, established actress in the play, and the older actress played the younger, supposedly sweeter, and inexperienced actress. The scene as written consists of a series of traded and escalating insults, threats, admissions, and confessions intended to put the other character off guard at the least, and feel defeated at the most. As the class watched, we heard several funny lines that did not have the power to make us laugh, and many that simply fell flat altogether. Most of the class did not recognize the scene as a comedy at all.

Neither did the actors. When polled, neither of the actors thought she was in a comedy, though both admitted that they thought certain things they said were funny. However, neither actor made any effort to use the funny things said in a way that would do anything but bury the humor. This would be no crime if the actors had other, more interesting things to do with their lines and with the unfolding situation of the scene. Unfortunately, one of the problems with the scene as presented was that neither actor seemed to know what was going on in the scene or between its two characters. This is not a good formula for success. So let's back up a bit and examine how this situation might have come to pass, and discuss how using the earlier list might have changed the situation.

The main problem in this scene was the failure of the actors to do two things. First, to recognize the kind of play they were in, and second, a failure to play what the scene was about. A familiarity with John Patrick Shanley's work would probably have told these actors that he likes to write plays about subcultures in our society. The offbeat characters he creates representing those subcultures produce both empathy and laughter in the audience because they are often funny and touching, as well as different than the audience who pays to watch them. In addition, the characters in a Shanley play are usually lacking something that they want very badly, and this generates the conflict in the play and in the characters.

This Shanley analysis holds up very well when examining *Four Dogs and a Bone.* Both women absolutely want to succeed in show business and, more specifically, in the picture they are currently making. They see each other as dangerous rivals, and because the older actress is more threatened, she takes the lead to destroy the other. The younger actress, though set up as "nicer," refuses to be cowed by the other and is left no choice but to engage in battle. The two women use every verbal device to destroy the other, including their ages, their talent, and their position relative to powerful men. In their verbal battle during the scene presented, there are victories, defeats, and discoveries aplenty. Because the characters go all out to destroy each other, the scene is absolutely life-and-death and hilarious, as well.

The actors playing the scene failed to consider the satirical world of the play—the exaggerated and cutthroat land of Hollywood, where success is everything. Understanding the play's world might have reinforced the conflict—the basic engine of drama—comedy or tragedy. In comedy, the higher the stakes for the character, the funnier the situation. The actress playing the younger character saw herself as nice and therefore chose not to engage in battle during the scene. Because she failed to do so, the conflict and the potential for hilarious nastiness and social commentary was debilitated.

Further, because of this miscue, the actors failed to use the dialogue, intended to flay the other character, as a weapon—therefore dulling the power of the language and, in turn, keeping the scene from being funny.

In addition, the scene that the actors brought in failed to use blocking to advantage, and as a result, their listening was compromised, as well. In the scene as first presented, there was a lot of aimless wandering across the stage. The scene was set in one of those trailers used during the filming of a movie. That kind of space is narrow and limited, an arrangement that would cause the conflict to be telescoped because of the lack of maneuverability. As a result, the characters would be forced into a face-to-face situation for much of the scene. This might have been used to great advantage in a scene about asserting and holding on to power. But because they failed to use space in this manner, their wandering physically kept them from listening to each other and from building on each previous adversarial comment.

Comic dialogue often operates in what I call the ladder pattern. One character says something, then is countered by the other, who in turn is countered again; one buildup on another until someone delivers the verbal knockout punch. A wisecrack to hurt, a powerful retort, a topping of the topper, and so forth. Language used as a weapon is integral to comedy where situations are life-and-death but where only the weapon of the tongue is available. Whenever the clincher line is delivered, there is a win and a loss, respectively, that causes a transitional moment. During that moment, each character is given the comedic opportunity to take stock of where she is, react, and find a new strategy for continuing the comedic war.

In summary, then, the actors in the *Four Dogs* scene had failed on their initial attempt at the scene to recognize the kind of play they were in and the style it required. This oversight set up a chain reaction of bad choices that led away from producing successful comedy. The actors had not thought of the play in terms of its inherent conflict, nor had they used the dialogue in the most effective manner. The language, as they had delivered it, was not used to obtain their objectives. Since they were not playing the conflict of the scene actively, there was no strong need to listen to each other and build on what was being said moment to moment. As a result, they did not use their blocking and physical action effectively and made choices that countered what was inherently funny about the situation and their characters. In short, we have here a textbook case of violating the rules of comedy. No wonder, then, that the audience did not laugh.

So, if you're acting in a comedy, be sure to do the following:

- Think in terms of conflict
- Use the dialogue to achieve your objective (use the funny in the words actively)
- Listen and react (make sure you react to what's funny and actively engage in the repartee of words)
- Use your physicality
- Don't step on what's funny in the script

On the positive side, immediately after we discussed the Shanley scene, the actors bravely agreed to rework it in front of the class. Immediately upon their starting to use the bullet points I just listed here, the scene became funny, extremely funny—without losing any of what the actors had hoped would be there. So, to some extent comedy is mathematical. The moral is, if you choose as an actor to make one and one add up to three, you are doomed to come up with an incorrect answer. But like those few old pleasures of algebra, if you come up with the right answers, when you go back to check your work, those answers plug in and prove to be a balanced equation every time.

The actors working on *Private Lives* also explained why they had chosen their scene and what they were hoping to get from working on it. They explained that they had chosen the scene because they had never done Coward and were interested in tackling this kind of material. The "style" frightened them a bit, they said, but the challenge also drew them to it. They explained that the British idioms and the accents were a problem, but they had been trying to work around their discomfort and deal with the language during their rehearsals. One of the pair contradicted this assertion, however, by saying he had tried to ignore the Britishness as much as possible in order to get comfortable with the scene. When the cutting was actually presented, the accents seemed more implied than actually there, and faded in and out as the scene progressed. This proved to be a minor distraction for those of us watching. But far more distracting was the fact that we could tell that the scene was supposed to be funny and was not. Although there were many funny and/or witty lines delivered, rather than making us laugh, those lines quietly traveled from our ears to our brains as a little voice inside us said, "Yes, a funny line indeed." Unfortunately, their work failed to produce anything physical or emotional in us as an audience. The scene had very little arc or throughline, and though it was not very long, it seemed to be so.

The first principle violated in the mounting of this scene was the one regarding genre and style. *Genre,* of course, refers to the category of play being presented. A comedy has certain characteristics, including being funny. Unlike in the other scene, the actors here were well aware that a Coward play is supposed to be funny, but at times they chose to play against the humor in order to make "real moments." Choosing to play against genre can be very dangerous, especially if going against the stream produces unsuccessful results. But comedy as a genre can also be broken down into more specific categories, such as farce, comedy of manners, character comedy, slapstick, and each of these subgroups has a set of comedic rules that are particular to its genre, including the style needed to make that genre work. The rules governing *style,* or, as it is sometimes defined, "the world of the play" must always be taken into consideration before acting choices can be made. A failure to do so can have particularly dire consequences.

Of course it is obvious that *Private Lives* is a comedy. The fact that it is by Noël Coward should tell us that immediately, as should a simple barebones reading of just the first few pages. The witty dialogue and the music of the lines should hit even the lamest reader squarely on the head with a sledgehammer. But if the lamest reader manages to miss that boat, he should have been protected by the fact that he had read up on one of the wittiest English-speaking playwrights of the twentieth century. A little research would have given the actor a cornucopia of information that could have been applied to the work required for this scene.

A little research tells us that Coward's plays are comedies of manners, also known as high-style comedies. These plays rely principally on wit, as expressed through their ingenious use of language. This type of play pokes fun at society's rules and customs. The pleasure in these plays for an audience comes through the characters' rapier-like wit, used to flay their fellow characters, and, as a byproduct, from the ribbing of the society in which these characters dwell. When Coward wrote, he was writing about the society in which he lived—the British middle and upper middle classes of seventy-plus years ago. This society had a set of ethics, rules of conduct, and manners far different than our own. The characters in a Coward play are of that particular world. They live by or violate this set of rules according to their wants and needs and according to the demands of the action of the play. The audience contemporary to that time understood the conventions of their time, as did the actors playing those characters. Today's audience does not necessarily comprehend that world, especially when the audience is American. Therefore, it is incumbent that the actors playing these roles come to understand those rules and operate according to them. Otherwise, a contemporary audience will never grasp them, nor be able to find the humor when those rules are purposely adhered to, violated, or poked fun at.

In the scene presented, Victor has discovered that the former husband of his new bride is in a hotel room next to his own honeymoon suite. After the plot has thickened a bit, Victor storms in on Elyot, the former husband of his Amanda, because he fears that Elyot is attempting to steal his bride from him. Jealous of the effect the former husband still has on his current wife, Victor has decided to fist-fight his rival. He fears that he will lose both Amanda and his manhood on this, his honeymoon. Sounds like a funny situation, no? In the scene as played, however, the actor playing the jealous husband, Victor, very quickly dropped the idea of battling for his wife and settled down instead to a very civilized conversation with Elyot on the subject. The scene turned out to have a lot of telling and very little doing. Before long, the exciting potential setup at the beginning of the scene stagnated and dried up.

Here's where understanding the world of the play becomes essential. High-class civilized gentlemen of the 1930s seldom reduced themselves to the level of barroom brawler by settling disputes with their fists. But Victor's extreme duress drives him to do so. Seeing him making such a spectacle of himself would be funny to the audience. The comic machinery here functions on a basic comic principle—the use of opposites. It is always funny when we see characters doing the opposite of what we expect of them. When actors keep this basic comedy principle in mind, as playwrights do, it will invariably open the door to far greater comic potential. People believably doing the opposite of what we expect of them will always lead to comic results.

In the situation between Elyot and Victor, we would laugh because the expectations of society are at odds with Victor's personal needs, and because we would soon see that Victor doesn't really want to fight; he just sees no other choice to protect his manhood. The comic situation would force Victor out of his own world, but unwillingly, since fighting is not something Victor really knows how to do or is comfortable with. As the scene progresses, Elyot's calm logic would further confuse Victor and make it difficult for him to maintain the level of hostility necessary to brawl with his rival. We would see Victor struggling to maintain his justified dudgeon, and we would see Elyot see it, as well. We would also see Elyot calmly and masterfully outbox Victor—with his tongue. By manipulating Victor with his use of wit, Elyot would manage to accomplish with his verbal gymnastics what Victor could not with his attempted physical efforts. The results, at least when read, are hilarious.

Unfortunately, this is not what we saw when the actors put up the scene for the first time. By failing to translate into their actions the world of the play, much of the basis for comedy was missed. We did not see Victor's absolute life-and-death need to regain his manhood through the uncivilized choice of fisticuffs, nor did we see how conflicted this impulse makes him. Instead of challenging Elyot physically, the actor playing Victor sat down almost immediately, taking away the threat in the scene. We therefore did not see how the cagey Elyot manipulates himself out of danger, so a battle of wits was quickly turned into a salon conversation. Neither of the actors actively used the Coward dialogue, dripping with wit, to fulfill their objectives. As a result, they blunted the dialogue's power in the scene and its laugh-producing potential for the audience. The fact that the British accents were not really present allowed the audience and the actors themselves to forget the time and place of the play, and the social conventions they imply. Further, the levels of character, demonstrated through wit and logic, was voided and the characters themselves flattened because the language was tossed off rather than used actively. Finally, because these cerebral men were not forced into an unnatural macho physicality, the potential for visual humor was blunted, as well.

All of these issues were discussed after the scene was presented, and like the actors in the other scene, the performers playing Elyot and Victor gamely jumped to their feet to make adjustments. Victor's simple act of bringing the need to fight onstage immediately turned everything around. The actor playing Victor was now hilarious, and his need forced the actor playing Elyot to have to deal with him as a legitimate problem rather than a speck of dust, easy to ignore. He now needed to work Victor out of his state while avoiding being bloodied. The stakes now present forced all the other elements to be dealt with actively, and the actors playing were now far better able to see what the audience sees, thus making each ensuing moment far richer than it had been before. The scene was well on its way to being solved.

In review, then, this scene demonstrated the following principles of acting comedy:

- A need to adhere to the rules governing the world of the play
- A need to be familiar with the playwright and how his material works whenever that is possible
- A need to find and play the conflict fully
- A use of language that supports the objectives being played
- A need to find physical choices that are funny and serve the objectives of the characters
- A need to play opposites when appropriate
- A need to support the actions of the scene without compromising what is inherently funny in it

Now that we have taken a look at two particular kinds of comedy, I should point out that there are other kinds of comedies, as well, and each of those, besides generally adhering to the principles already mentioned, requires adherence to its own particular characteristics. There are the contemporary realistic comedies of the mature Neil Simon, for instance. Or the character comedies of such authors as Beth Henley and Wendy Wasserstein. Or hilarious dark comedies brimming with social commentary by playwrights such as Christopher Durang and Nicky Silver. And then there are the farces, perfected a century ago by the great French playwright Georges Feydeau, whose tradition is carried along by such contemporary British playwrights as Michael Frayn and Alan Ayckbourn and here in America by Paul Rudnick, Ken Ludwig, and Larry Shue, among others.

A good example of character comedy is the Beth Henley play *Crimes of the Heart,* which many of you are probably familiar with. The action centers on three quirky sisters from a small town in Mississippi who are reunited because the youngest, sweetest, and dimmest of the three has inexplicably shot her husband in the stomach with the intent to kill him. This unlikely setup for comedy is funny because the characters are. Yet what makes the characters funny is not necessarily quick wit, a pratfall, or a situation so extreme that it drives its characters out of their normal behavior. Rather, it is the slow unfolding of who each character is, how each relates to the other characters, and how each deals in her unique fashion with the vagaries and vicissitudes that life has brought her. The truthful yet surprising reactions to the world that each displays are what make the audience laugh. In such a play, the actors must make believable and realistic choices for their characters just as they would in a drama, but they must be sure to have an awareness of what is funny about their characters and make sure that each moment, filled with discovery and new information, is fully realized. The physical characterizations of the offbeat characters in a play such as *Crimes of the Heart* must also be thought about and constructed specifically to maximize the humor generated by each character in the play.

A play by Neil Simon operates much like *Crimes of the Heart* does. However, the characters in a Simon play are aware of their senses of humor and their wit and, like the characters found in a comedy of manners, use their wit to get what they need. They enjoy their own senses of humor, and their verbal jousting is an active rather than passive activity. But unlike in a comedy of manners, the characters in a mature Neil Simon play are, for the most part, multidimensional, and their complexity and truthfulness draw us, more than any plot devices or attempted social commentary. The comedy, therefore, is generated from who the characters are and what they need rather than by any sudden twist and turn of the plot. But clearly, even though character-centered, a Simon play is filled with funny dialogue and capped with punch lines that must be respected by properly setting them up and effectively using the dialogue as written. This requires more than a come-what-may attitude to the mechanics of the wordplay. The actors must respect the dialogue by using it with an understanding of how it is structured and used by the characters—if they are to get the comic results expected.

A play by Christopher Durang or Nicky Silver is another comic hybrid that combines elements of various comedic subgroups. In a Durang play we find the biting social satire of a comedy of manners and the conscious and active use of wit by characters to get what they need as in a Simon play, but the world in which the Durang characters live is a bizarro place—uglier and more twisted than the everyday world we all inhabit. As a result, the characters have also been twisted into satirical extremes of the people who populate our society. Their wants and needs have been malformed in accordance with the twisted logic they have learned from their twisted world. Yet for them, that world is as real as the one we live in.

Playing this exaggerated world in an exaggerated fashion is an understandable but ineffective acting choice to make, however. What does make a Durang play work effectively is an absolute commitment to the reality of that world without any commenting by the actors to show how ridiculous they, as actors, think it is. The script itself provides all the craziness needed. When the actors keep it real by truthfully adhering to the life-and-death needs of their characters, the comedic potential and the satirical underpinnings are most successfully realized.

And finally, a word or two about farce, a category of comedy whose definition goes a long way toward telling actors how it should be played. Farce might be described as a comic play in which the laughs are produced through the broad, ridiculous choices of its characters, where the comedy is physical and mostly produced as a result of the plot rather than via character or witty dialogue. Characters in a farce find themselves in what they consider to be absolute life-and-death situations. As a result, they are willing to do anything and everything to extricate themselves from the fix in which they find themselves. Obviously, in this kind of comedy the actor must be willing to make the most extreme choices, because the character he or she is playing would. In this world, *extreme* is the operative word. Plays such as *Noises Off* or movies such as *Rat Race* or classic Marx Brothers films are fine examples of both this genre and the style required to pull this genre off. *Madcap* is an adjective that might describe all the required choices that must be made by actors for this kind of play. Only when the actors commit to the extremes provided by the play, physically and emotionally, do the mechanics of a farce fall into place and start humming.

In summary, then, comedy is a specialized brand of acting. But it is not out of the reach of actors willing to do the work required to make it successful. Knowing the world of the play and converting that understanding into choices that will make the audience laugh is not so much a matter of talent as it is of doing the work necessary to produce those laughs. Research into the world of the play and an understanding of the rules governing the genre and style of a play will go a long way toward getting you the results you desire. There are countless superb DVD's sitting on the shelves awaiting rental that can demonstrate in action many, if not all, of the principles put forth in this chapter. Why not take the time to see how each operates, and begin building that arsenal of comedic skills? No doubt there's a laugh or two waiting for you as payment for your hard work.

CHAPTER SIX

ACTING SHAKESPEARE

YOU HAVE PROBABLY FIGURED OUT BY NOW THAT I believe that an actor's primary purpose is to tell the story of the play clearly, compellingly, and believably. That means your focus should first and foremost be directed on playing actions, not on character or emotions. That means you should be using the words chosen by the playwright to get what your character needs, rather than to reveal character traits, emotional underpinning, underlying symbolism, or hidden meaning. When you use dialogue and actions to tell the story of the play, miraculously, the play itself communicates character, symbol, and underlying meaning. If you do your work regarding dialogue and action, the other elements will make themselves clear. Figurative language and the great idea are always better understood when connected to the story context in which they are used or developed. Be careful not to fall into the trap of playing an idea, or focusing on character rather than story, emotion rather than action.

This caveat is particularly important to remember when working on Shakespeare. There is an assumption that as we read a play by the bard, we automatically absorb the developing plot elements and that we understand how new events, information, and discoveries affect character, relationship, and basic need. But that is seldom the case. When Romeo finds out that Juliet is a Capulet, we practically take for granted the effect such information has on character, plot, and the resulting dialogue. Very little dialogue is given to Romeo to express his thoughts and feelings when, at the Capulet masque, he finds out who this ravishing young woman is, but there is no doubt that this knowledge profoundly affects his subsequent actions. When the freshly honored Macbeth returns home after being told by the witches that he is to be king, he has no intention of killing Duncan. Yet in one brief scene, his wife manages to completely turn him around. How is that accomplished? The written dialogue offers some clues but no answers. We usually just take for granted that it happens. But why? The "how it happens" is what is interesting in the situation. It is what is most watchable, and the choices about how it is accomplished onstage give life to the words and actions that the audience sees and hears. The implications of dialogue and action become your responsibility to make clear to the audience. It is you who must make tangible what is implied in the script.

What we take for granted as readers and watchers often goes to the very core of what makes a play interesting to an audience. Without connecting the dialogue of the play to the essential elements of the play's action—the action that inspires the language—the words can remain for actors and audience, for that matter, as inaccessible and cold as a distant mountain peak, beautiful to look at, perhaps, but hardly worth an expedition. As actors, you must be willing to make that dangerous climb.

I love the conceit presented in the film *Shakespeare in Love*—that Shakespeare as a young playwright was trying to whip together some plays that work, so that he could sell them to some producer and get his rent paid. No self-aware poetic genius at work here, just a struggling dramatist working with the elements he had studied and seen work onstage previously. The fact that his body of dramatic work proved to be that of a staggering genius of language, character, and the human condition should not distract us as actors from the simple truth that his plays work and function like the dramatic entities they are. If you learn to approach Shakespeare with this conceit in mind, the other aspects that we often focused on first in English class will come across even more effectively on their own.

Because Shakespeare is word driven, you analysis must start with the words. Here follows a basic list of the things you must consider when preparing to take on the language of Shakespeare:

- A literal analysis for meaning of the words individually and together, including definitions, ideas contained therein, literary and historical allusion, and poetic language and imagery
- An analysis of the words as a result of the specific dramatic circumstances in which they are said
- An analysis of all dramatic events leading up to a particular scene or section of dialogue so as to understand the speech in the overall dramatic context in which it is being said

Now here is an example of how these three analysis tools might work on a piece of dialogue. Below is the opening line spoken by the character Antonio in *The Merchant of Venice.*

\In sooth, I know not why I am so sad.\

I appropriated the use of this line from the television series and subsequent book called *Playing Shakespeare,* which featured director John Barton and members of the Royal Shakespeare Company. This series of programs on how to do Shakespeare can be of enormous benefit to you as an actor. The programs, recently released on DVD, are expensive and maybe somewhat difficult to find, but the book based on the programs is easy to come by and offers a wonderful opportunity to observe how expert actors think about and make their choices with the language of Shakespeare. If you can get your hands on either or both, you will be well served.

Antonio's statement is a good line to start with. The words are all one syllable and, except for the word "sooth," their literal meanings well known. You might try this as an opening exercise on your own. To start with, simply repeat the line as many ways as you can. You will be amazed at the variety of readings you can produce, as a result of some emotional connotation you supply and/or by the word or words you choose to emphasize. Some of your readings will be more effective than others simply because they sound better to the ear—a result of respecting the meter (repetition of stresses found in the line). Don't worry; this will be detailed later.

Think about which readings you liked best, and try to determine why you think what you think. Now try reading the line aloud again, emphasizing a particular word. The italics in the following repeats of the line represent possible words that might be stressed.

In *sooth,* I know not why I am so sad.
In sooth, I *know* not why I am so sad.
In sooth, I know not *why* I am so sad.
In sooth, I know not why I *am* so sad.
In sooth, I know not why I am so *sad.*

Each of the readings, with the exception, perhaps, of the line with the *know* emphasis, probably gave off a specific meaning and sounded well to the ear. By emphasizing *sooth,* you seem to be confessing to not knowing why you are so sad. By emphasizing the *why,* you seem to be acknowledging that you have no explanation for your mood. By emphasizing the *am* (a weak choice because verbs of being tend not to carry much meaning), you seem to be agreeing that you are sad and are confessing that you don't know the reason why you feel as you do. Finally, by emphasizing the *sad,* you seem to be discovering in the moment that you are sad.

All of these readings of the line are possible good choices. In a dramatic vacuum, each would work nicely. But what if you are to speak the line in the context of the play? That's where dramatic analysis comes into action. Again, no one answer is correct, but your choices would be narrowed by the provided context. If, for instance, Antonio had just been asked, "Why are you so sad?" then his answer might very well emphasize *sooth* or *why,* or both *sooth* and *why.*

Now say the line as though you are answering a particular question or set of questions, or better still, find someone to actually ask you something. The responses that sound right will be the ones that acknowledge the question in your answer. You will find that the emphasized words in the answer will change in accordance with the question you are asked—if you are really listening. That, of course, is always a key element in making the speaking of Shakespeare, or any other dramatic work, for that matter, work effectively. You've always got to remember to listen and react.

Now suppose that we know more about the dramatic context of the chosen line. Set up the following scenarios before reading the line again.

- A party where everyone is underage and has been drinking
- A private discussion with a family member who has done something wrong (be specific)
- A private discussion with a lover who has cheated
- A conversation with a priest, teacher, therapist who is trying to give help
- Other

You get the idea. Each of these suggestions should affect the way you deliver the line and give it a specific color—color that might not have been there if your analysis of the specific and overall dramatic context had not been considered. It is not enough that you are able to get through the lines clearly. You must also bring along a knowledge of the situation. For instance, consider what you must know when Juliet says in act 3, scene 2 of *Romeo and Juliet* the following:

> Gallop apace, you fiery-footed steeds,
> Towards Phoebus' lodging; such a wagoner
> As Phaeton would whip you to the west,
> And bring in cloudy night immediately.

The reader of these lines must know the literal meaning of the words, the mythical references used to construct the poetic figurative language, the situation at hand, and the reason for Juliet's wanting the fiery-footed steeds to pull that sun-laden wagon. In short, you must consider how badly Juliet wants night to arrive—so that the time of Romeo's arrival will be at hand. All of this is fairly obvious, but too often in your preparation, you may ignore the obvious. As a result you miss the opportunities to bring genuine excitement to the performance. By doing the work, you will learn about the poetic structure contained within the lines, and you will be pulled along by the pulsing drama contained within them. Obviously, as an actor, this is what you want to do.

Now let's return for just a moment to that earlier speech by Antonio. Here again is the opening line to *The Merchant of Venice* with some other stressed words that you might have heard during the earlier exercise.

In sooth, I know not why I am so sad.
In sooth, *I* know not why I am so sad.
In sooth, I know *not* why I am so sad.
In sooth, I know not why *I* am so sad.
In sooth, I know not why I am *so* sad.

Notice that when you choose to emphasize these words, the lines sit poorly on the ear and seem to provide less clarity to the meaning of the line? That is because the stressing of those particular words don't provide enough clarity. The ear tells us that. But suppose that you don't at this point have an ear sophisticated enough to hear that. You can still depend on the natural stressing of the line. This line is written in *iambic pentameter.* Every other syllable is stressed—second, fourth, and so on. All of Shakespeare's verse generally adheres to this rhythm, and a simple reading for the stressed syllables, or *scansion,* can help you get clues as to what should or should not be emphasized. Of course, Shakespeare doesn't always stick exactly to the format. If he did, the lines would be so rhythmic that they would sound like a children's verse. But when he does violate the regular pattern, he always does so for a reason. Of the four lines above, only the one with the *not* emphasis has a clear meaning. The violation of the natural rhythm works, because it emphasizes a possible meaning of the line. The question, one that we will save for another time, is whether the violation works better than one of the other, earlier readings that did follow the natural rhythm of the line.

The reference to scansion suggests that there are other rules or guidelines that you can also learn—rules that will help you read Shakespeare more clearly and effectively. Actually, there are several. None of them is difficult, and with a little practice and help, they can be mastered quickly. Once you can utilize these tools, effective readings will quickly become the rule rather than the exception. Here is a list for you to consider:

- Scansion
- Punctuation—obey the traffic signs
- Determining operative words—circle and emphasize the words that best communicate the meaning of an idea, phrase, or sentence
- Notation and use of verbs
- Maintaining energy at the ends of lines—don't drop the energy at the end of a line unless it is also the end of an idea, phrase, or sentence

- Phrasing—breaking sentences into idea units
- Caesura—using idea breaks to help the line make sense
- Breathing—do it according to the punctuation
- Transitions—making a vocal shift when there is an idea shift
- Apposition and antithesis—making vocal use of opposites
- Alliteration—using it vocally

Now let's take a look at an actual scene from the play *Macbeth.* The purpose here is to demonstrate that the basic elements of drama—plot, character, dialogue, and idea—that seem so obvious when performed well onstage seem far less so when you are reading the words on the page. And in order for you to make the scene come alive, you will have to develop the skills that successful actors use when performing Shakespeare.

READING FOR THE STORY

Let's begin by reading the scene that follows just for meaning. If you were my own students, I would also ask you to jot down any words or phrases that you're not sure about. It might be a good idea for you to do so. You're liable to be surprised at what you thought you knew but don't.

THE TRAGEDY OF MACBETH

ACT 1, SCENE 5

[*Enter* Lady Macbeth, *with a letter*]

Lady Macbeth: [*reading*] "They met me in the day of success,
and I have learned by the perfect'st report they have
more in them than mortal knowledge. When I burned in
desire to question them further, they made themselves
air, into which they vanished. Whiles I stood rapt in the
wonder of it came missives from the King, who all-hailed
me 'Thane of Cawdor', by which title before these weird
sisters saluted me, and referred me to the coming on of

time with 'Hail, King that shalt be!' This have I thought good to deliver thee, my dearest partner of greatness, that thou mightst not lose the dues of rejoicing by being ignorant of what greatness is promised thee. Lay it to thy heart, and farewell."

Glamis thou art, and Cawdor, and shalt be
What thou art promised. Yet do I fear thy nature.
It is too full o' th' milk of human kindness
To catch the nearest way. Thou wouldst be great,
Art not without ambition, but without
The illness should attend it. What thou wouldst highly,
That wouldst thou holily; wouldst not play false,
And yet wouldst wrongly win. Thou'dst have, great Glamis,

That which cries "Thus thou must do" if thou have it,
And that which rather thou dost fear to do
Than wishest should be undone. Hie thee hither,
That I may pour my spirits in thine ear
And chastise with the valour of my tongue
All that impedes thee from the golden round
Which fate and metaphysical aid doth seem
To have thee crowned withal.

[*Enter a* SERVANT]

What is your tidings?

SERVANT: The King comes here tonight.
LADY MACBETH: Thou'rt mad to say it.
Is not thy master with him, who, were 't so,
Would have informed for preparation?
SERVANT: So please you, it is true. Our thane is coming,
One of my fellows had the speed of him,
Who, almost dead for breath, had scarcely more
Than would make up his message.
LADY MACBETH: Give him tending;
He brings great news.

[*Exit Servant*]

The raven himself is hoarse
That croaks the fatal entrance of Duncan
Under my battlements. Come, you spirits
That tend on mortal thoughts, unsex me here,
And fill me from the crown to the toe top-full
Of direst cruelty. Make thick my blood,
Stop up th' access and passage to remorse,
That no compunctious visitings of nature
Shake my fell purpose, nor keep peace between
Th' effect and it. Come to my woman's breasts,
And take my milk for gall, you murd'ring ministers,
Wherever in your sightless substances
You wait on nature's mischief. Come, thick night,
And pall thee in the dunnest smoke of hell,
That my keen knife see not the wound it makes,
Nor heaven peep through the blanket of the dark
To cry "Hold, hold!"

[*Enter* MACBETH]

Great Glamis, worthy Cawdor,
Greater than both by the all-hail hereafter,
Thy letters have transported me beyond
This ignorant present, and I feel now
The future in the instant.

MACBETH: My dearest love,
Duncan comes here tonight.
LADY MACBETH: And when goes hence?
MACBETH: Tomorrow, as he purposes.
LADY MACBETH: O never
Shall sun that morrow see.
Your face, my thane, is as a book where men
May read strange matters. To beguile the time,
Look like the time; bear welcome in your eye,

Your hand, your tongue; look like the innocent flower,
But be the serpent under 't. He that's coming
Must be provided for; and you shall put
This night's great business into my dispatch,
Which shall to all our nights and days to come
Give solely sovereign sway and masterdom.

MACBETH: We will speak further.

LADY MACBETH: Only look up clear.
To alter favour ever is to fear.
Leave all the rest to me.

[*Exeunt*]

I suspect that if I asked you what happened in the scene above, your answer would be extremely interesting but probably less than accurate. If you had read the play up to this scene before taking on act 1, scene 5, you would probably do better than if you had just read scene out of context. But even had you read the scene in the context of the play up to this point, the language may have prevented you from understanding it.

The words in the context of the play, and the context of the play reflecting on the words, intersect to provide meaning. Without a specific understanding of that meaning, you will probably flounder. Whether you should start with a general understanding of the scene's dramatic progression or an examination of the language can be debated. But I have found it far easier to start with the action, and then bring in the language once the groundwork of the scene has been established. It will help you to understand the specifics of the language.

The most effective way of getting to the story of the scene is to focus on the plot—that is the literal chronological action that is essentially a cause-and-effect process. The plot, which is so obvious when an audience sees it done onstage before them, is often far more deceptive when sitting quietly on a printed page. Dramatic points of interest that are absolutely clear when performed are often missed altogether when read and performed only in the theatre of your mind—and especially if the language is alien, as Shakespeare certainly is for many actors.

An effective way of getting to the heart of the action is to accurately list on paper the cause-and-effect chronology of a scene. You must use the text to find and support any event you choose to list. You may find that you have a great deal of difficulty isolating the action of a scene from its other elements. You may want to mix character description, given circumstances, and your personal interpretation of what is going on in the scene all together. The challenge is to stick to cause-and-effect actions—the essentials of making the scene work actively.

Your exploration should always begin with the overall chronology of the play—the given circumstances to this point—but for our purposes here we'll jump right to the chronology of the scene above.

The actual cause-and-effect list of plot action that you ultimately come up with might look something like this:

At the opening of act 1, scene 5, Lady Macbeth is reading a letter sent her by her husband. At the point the action picks up, she is reading of his encounter with the Weird Sisters. She reads his description of their supernatural power to predict the future and their sudden disappearance into thin air. Through implication we see that Lady Macbeth already knows of her husband's victory and heroic action. ("They met me in the day of success.") She learns of the arrival of messengers who report of Macbeth's promotion and of the witches' prediction that Macbeth will become king.

After finishing the letter, Lady Macbeth declares that Macbeth will be king. However, she realizes his character is such that it may prevent him from doing what is necessary to get the crown. She beckons Macbeth home so that she might pour her courage into his ear and convince him to do what is necessary to become king.

A messenger then enters and reports to her that the king will arrive that very night. Lady Macbeth suggests her murderous thoughts by declaring that the messenger is mad to have said such a thing. Quickly recovering, she praises the messenger for having brought great news and dismisses him. When alone, Lady Macbeth begins a soliloquy in which she hints that the king will soon be dead and conjures spirits of evil to stop up any weakness that being a woman might cause her to have. She enlists the help of the spirits to do what must be done with the murderous knife she will use.

At that moment, Macbeth enters. They see each other. It is the wife who speaks first, by flattering her husband with alluring titles old and new and suggesting that greater titles await. Macbeth responds by saying the king comes there that night. Lady Macbeth asks when the king is to leave, and her husband responds, "tomorrow," but adds with great implication "as he purposes." Lady Macbeth then reveals her heart by telling her husband that the king will not live until tomorrow. Macbeth's face betrays his doubts and fear, but his wife quickly instructs him to hide his feelings, lest they give him away. She further instructs him to leave the rest to her. Macbeth wants to speak further, but his wife silences him with a repeated warning that he must look innocent and once again instructs him to leave all plans to her. They exit together.

Here is an even more concise version:

- Lady Macbeth reads her husband's letter.
- The contents of the letter cause her to declare that Macbeth will be king.
- The declaration causes her to realize that her husband has traits that will prevent his doing what he needs to.
- This realization causes her to beckon him home so that she can mold him into shape.
- A messenger interrupts with news that the king is coming.
- This news causes Lady M to blurt out an incriminating comment about her murderous intent.
- Having said the remark causes her to cover the moment so the servant doesn't catch on and further causes her get rid of him as quickly as possible.
- Being alone again causes her to take the opportunity to conjure evil spirits to help her with her murderous plot.
- Macbeth's entrance causes her to be interrupted.
- Macbeth's arrival causes Lady Macbeth to face her husband for the first time. Seeing him causes her to start manipulating him, first using titles that will appeal to him.
- Hearing his wife's praise causes Macbeth to inform her that the king will come that night.
- Hearing this causes his wife to ask when the king will leave.
- Hearing his answer causes her to begin to reveal her plan for murder.
- Hearing her suggested plan causes Macbeth to try to stop her.
- His attempt at stopping her causes her to take over and insist that he leave everything to her.
- Macbeth is convinced by his wife to let her take charge, and the couple leaves together.

The story of the scene is a good one indeed. During its short duration, two people, still highly respected by the world, begin to consider actions that are evil and that will irrevocably change their lives and who they are forever. A wife suddenly takes on the role and power of husband, and a husband is suddenly dumbfounded and controlled by a wife. Both are about to begin a journey that even moments before they never would have thought possible.

Though the scene on the printed page consists only of dialogue, the story summarized here is primarily told in terms of actions, or, in other words, in terms of what the characters do. The fact is, when read with a proper dramatic perspective, dialogue is primarily about doing. Any good actor must think in these terms. Dialogue is about characters using words to fulfill needs—needs that can be met either by another character who is present or, as in the case of Lady Macbeth's soliloquy, by entities who are not.

Notice that I have carefully selected action verbs to describe what goes on in the scene—because well-selected verbs suggest action rather than feelings, and the dramatic progression of a scene depends on its action. The verbs you will find in my description include *reads, learns, declares, realizes, beckons, recovers, praises, dismisses, conjures, enlists, exchange, flatters, reveals, betrays, instructs, silences,* and *warns.* Each of these verbs suggests a playable action, and actors who take their cues from these verbs and do what the verbs suggest will collect a lot of mileage toward making even a reading of this scene interesting.

There are several moments that I have put into the story that have not been referenced in the dialogue, yet they are as important to the story as the spoken dialogue. For instance, the moment Macbeth and his wife first see each other at the top of the scene. Given all that has happened to him, including a prediction of future greatness, and all that she has said in the previous moments, what must their exchanged looks reveal or conceal? Then, at the end of the scene, the future king and queen exit together. What is it that Lady Macbeth has said to her husband, or better yet, done to him, that allows this warrior hero to accept her leadership in a plan that is about to lead to murder? The answers to these questions are an integral part of the scene.

I have also included several dramatic moments that are suggested through the dialogue but not dwelled on. Lady Macbeth's references to Macbeth's facial expressions indicate what Macbeth's thoughts and actions are, even though he has no specific dialogue to support them. "Oh never shall sun that morrow see" must no doubt produce quite a reaction to the previously unsuspecting thane of Cawdor. With practice, a careful actor reading for story progression will soon learn to recognize these kinds of dramatic moments. And this, of course, is the goal of this kind of process. More to the point, it is something that you must learn to do.

If you are not the best reader, then obviously Shakespeare poses an additional challenge to your already challenged self. As an actor you must be able to read a script effectively. Consider it your ongoing homework to improve, if that is the case. If Shakespeare seems totally inaccessible to you, try reading a version of the play that includes a summary of the action. There are versions that give an overall summary, an act summary, and a scene-by-scene summary. If you need this kind of help, don't be ashamed to use it. Ultimately, you will be judged on what you produce, not on the mechanics of how you get there. Do what you need to in order to do the best work you can.

As you tackle a scene to find its cause-and-effect arc or throughline of action, you will quickly discover that plot is a lot more difficult to spell out than it appears when you watch a play unfold. In fact, turning dialogue into specific actions can be messy work once you begin the process. It is easy to miss significant action moments and even easier to misinterpret what is being said by a character. The most efficient way to overcome these analytical obstacles is to start at the end of the scene and work backward. Cause and effect become quite clear when you turn it into effect and cause. Try starting with "exeunt" and work your way back to "enter," and you will quickly become believers.

ANALYZING THE LANGUAGE

Now it's time to examine the dialogue of the scene. Remember, I asked you to jot down the words and phrases you weren't sure about. Were you my students, I would also have asked you to look up the meanings of every word or phrase you had jotted down. The best way to make sure you do this effectively is to use a carefully annotated version of the play and, for convenience, one that makes the commentary easily accessible. I prefer the ones like Folger or Signet, which have the commentary right on the page or on the page adjoining.

It is essential that you look up the meaning of every word you do not know. That may mean many additional words that were not annotated in your playbooks. You need to remember that in the four hundred years since Shakespeare wrote them, the meaning and usage of words may have changed, and in some cases changed a great deal. If you are dealing with words not annotated, be sure you examine archaic meanings as well as the meaning they currently hold. The differences, by the way, can be quite stark and change totally the meaning of a line.

If you consider this process detective work through which exciting discoveries can be made, the task at hand will seem sexy rather than amount to drudgery. Just keep reminding yourself that in order to make the scene come alive, you will have to know exactly what the characters are saying and meaning when they say it. You can do that only by taking the time to really think about the words being used. I can't emphasize enough the importance of never assuming. If you have any doubts about the meaning of a word or phrase, you must look it up.

Here is a list I compiled while rereading the scene above. With the words and phrases that held particular interest for me, I have included what I found when I looked them up, or I have commented on their implications. Some of the words and phrases, when checked against the references I used, became deeper, more interesting, or more poetically complex than I might first have realized. In every case the meanings provided made the material more interesting and more dramatically useful than I initially suspected. The meanings also helped explain or amplified the reasons that the playwright chose a particular alliteration in a particular phrase.

"day of success"—victory in battle, a suggestion by the playwright that Lady M already has read of Macbeth's performance in battle

"perfect'st report"—the accuracy of the report they gave; suggests their supernatural abilities

"missives"—messengers (not messages, as I first thought)

"weird"—of or relating to fate, a more specific meaning than the "weird" we know today

"nearest way"—easiest, or the way that is most available

"illness should attend it"—evil quality (ruthlessness) that might go with great ambition

"highly/holily"—(use of H sound emphasizes a comparison here)

"wouldst wrongly win"—would be willing to win unfairly; again, alliteration for emphasis

"hie thee hither"—alliterative H sounds suggest speed

"chastise/valor of my tongue"—scold with my tongue, which is not afraid to say anything

"golden round"—crown

"metaphysical"—supernatural

"seem . . . withal"—that fate seems to have already given you

"raven /hoarse"—raven as symbol of death combined with croaking and hoarse make an almost funny yet horrific image

"fatal"—meaning here directed by fate rather than its contemporary meaning, but certainly deadly for the about-to-be-murdered king

"unsex"—a frightening image implying losing all the things that give her feminine qualities

"make thick my blood"—a thickened blood was believed to result in a ferocity of disposition

"compunctious"—compassionate

"fell purpose"—fierce and savage

"take my milk for gall"—a gruesome antithetical image (more on antithesis later)

"thick night"—besides the normal usage, *thick* also means morally corrupt

"pall"—enshroud

"dunnest"—darkest

"keen knife"—besides sharp, *keen* also means bitter and eager "beguile"—deceive

"solely sovereign sway"—alliteration for effect (more on alliteration later)

"alter favor ever is to fear"—to look other than normal will cause you to feel that people may be on to you

SKILLS FOR READING ALOUD

Now that we have examined the action of the scene and the meaning of the language, let's take a look at some of the skills necessary for reading Shakespeare aloud effectively. We'll begin with what I consider the two most important: using the punctuation, and identifying the operative words—the words that carry the most meaning in a phrase, line, or sentence.

PUNCTUATION AND OTHER TRAFFIC SIGNS

I often tell my own students that punctuation in a play by Shakespeare is like an organized system of traffic signs. If you obey the signs, you will reach your destination (or clarity of meaning) safely. If you fail to obey the signs, you will end up getting lost or having an accident. All those archaic words and figures of speech piled up on the page like cars at rush hour demand the use of traffic signs to prevent potential reading chaos.

The traffic rules are really quite simple. You learned them in grade school. Periods indicate the end of whole ideas and require a stop. A stop, by the way, is always a good place to take a necessary breath. Commas indicate a slighter pause and usually suggest a shift of idea or a slight turn in another direction, but not a complete ending of a particular idea. If a breath is necessary, you should take a short one. The ends of lines require you to follow the punctuation. If there's no traffic sign, then the idea continues on to the next line, and so does your energy—until another traffic sign appears. This means that unless there is a sign, there must be no dip in energy at the end of a line. In fact, it is not unusual for the end of a line to contain an important word, if not *the* most important word in that line.

Too often, American actors take pauses wherever they feel the acting urge to do so. They like to make moments. But this can be dramatic suicide when acting Shakespeare. Verse has a rhythm and music of its own that become apparent when read aloud with some degree of understanding. Stops and pauses are ingeniously built in by Mr. Shakespeare. He tells you if and when a pause is necessary. Shakespeare and his early editors knew where their dramatic bread was buttered. Seldom will you be able to buck the system and make a better reading than the one suggested by the provided punctuation. An unnecessary pause can kill the beauty and clarity of a line by Shakespeare. So can ignoring pauses when they should be there.

There are a few more subtle traffic signs written on the Shakespearean page, and these involve the structure of the verse form that Shakespeare used. Shakespearean verse is written in iambic pentameter, as stated earlier. When we get to scansion in a few moments, we'll talk about this in more detail. Iambic pentameter means that in a regular line (a line that does not break its established rhythm pattern) there will be five repetitions of an unstressed syllable, followed by a stressed syllable. There is no magic here. Our language is made up of words in which some syllables are accented or stressed, and some are not. Here is an example:

Thy **let** /ters **have**/ tran**sport**/ed **me**/ be**yond**/

This is a *regular line.* Each unstressed syllable is followed by a stressed one five times. Sometimes, however, a spoken line is left uncompleted by one speaker and the next speaker finishes the *pentameter* (five repetitions of a pattern) on the next line. Here is an example of lines being completed by multiple actors:

MACBETH: My dearest love,
Duncan comes here tonight.
LADY MACBETH: **And when goes hence?**
MACBETH: Tomorrow, as he purposes.
LADY MACBETH: **O never**
Shall sun that morrow see.
Your face, my thane, is as a book where men
May read strange matters. To beguile the time,

Notice how in lines 3 and 5, Lady Macbeth completes the pentameter that Macbeth has begun. Since the pentameter has purposely been uncompleted in Macbeth's speech, the reader may assume that the author intended for Lady M to complete the missing beats. It also suggests that Lady M comes right in with her lines. This, of course, when properly executed, gives the effect that Lady M is energized and taking control of the conversation. On the other hand, notice how the sixth line is left uncompleted just after Lady Macbeth lays down her bombshell. Since the line is intentionally left incomplete, it suggests that there is a long pause during which Macbeth produces the physical reaction to which Lady Macbeth refers in the next line. These are the kinds of traffic signs my high school teachers never told me about, but I certainly would have been fascinated had they approached the play as you must if you are an actor.

I learned a simpler way of looking at stresses in a line from a colleague—a brilliant professor of English Renaissance poetry. He told me to forget about the unstressed syllables and patterns. He said just find five stresses in the line and you've got it licked. If you find a *spondee* (two stressed syllables back to back), he added, then count it as one stress. You'll find that this system usually works. And when you find the stresses, it is a big hint toward finding the operative words.

FINDING AND USING OPERATIVE WORDS

Now let's move on to operative words—the words that help to convey the meaning and dramatic purpose of each spoken line. When you learn to identify the operative words in a piece of dialogue, you will have taken a major step toward reading Shakespeare with clarity and dramatic insight. When this knowledge is used in combination with a healthy regard for the traffic signs on the page, you may become a serious threat to the Oliviers and Branaughs who are able to make a living from the skill.

So, how do you identify the words that most convey meaning and that move the action forward? A good way to start is by using scansion—the scanning of lines to determine where the naturally occurring accented syllables are. Let's take a look.

Come, thick night,
And **pall** / thee **in** / the **dun** /nest **smoke** / of **hell,** /
That **my** / keen **knife** / see **not** / the **wound** / it **makes**, /

Nor **hea** / ven **peep** / through the **blan** / ket **of** / the **dark** /
To **cry** / **"Hold, hold!"** /

In this climactic moment from Lady Macbeth's conjuring-of-evil speech, you will notice that the second and third lines scan regularly. As explained earlier, these lines are written in a normal *iambic* (unstressed syllable followed by stressed) pattern. But lines 1, 4, and 5 do not scan perfectly. As a result of the natural stresses in a line in conjunction with their dramatic context, we get clear hints as to what syllables or words should be hit harder than others. In line 2, we see that *pall, in, dun* (from *dunnest*), *smoke,* and *hell* are all accented. In line 3 we see that *my, knife, not, wound,* and *makes* get the stresses. It then becomes an interesting detective game to further rank the words according to their usefulness. There are no absolute right or wrongs, but by going through this process you will begin an evaluative journey that will ultimately help you read the lines effectively.

Let's examine lines 2 and 3 further. In line 2 there is the verb *pall.* Verbs suggest action, and we already know that in drama action is everything. In general, verbs are important dramatic meaning conveyers. Therefore *pall* is a useful word and definitely should be hit hard. Ends of lines also require an energy to keep the sense ongoing into the next line, so *hell* is also important. *Smoke* is stressed, so it is next in order of importance—because *dunnest* is archaic (and therefore carries no meaning for a contemporary ear)—and smoke of hell combine to make a phrase that creates a strong image. *In* is only a preposition, which does not carry a lot of power. *In* will be hit slightly, simply because of the natural rhythm of the line. Circle *pall, smoke,* and *hell* on your script. Now reread the line aloud, stressing your circled words. The line probably sounded pretty good, didn't it?

Go through the same process with line 3. A lot of room for discussion here. But my picks are *makes, wound, not,* and *knife*, in that order. *Makes* because verbs carry action, *wound* because it's a great image, *not* because in combination with the unstressed "sees" it creates a coldheartedness in the speaker that is dramatically effective. If your order is different than mine, try it a few ways aloud and see what works best. You may find that you love saying the lines aloud trying the words in different combinations of stress to make a dramatic impact. The ultimate result is that you will develop an appreciation for the words themselves and how you can use them.

The first line, because of the combination of one-syllable words, comes out slow and sharply staccato. It is hard to say one-syllable words one after another too quickly, and there are no unaccented syllables between them to relax on. Dramatically, this means all the words are hit hard. Try saying the line aloud. Pretty powerful, huh? Now say it like you're really conjuring, as Lady M is. What do you think?

Lines 4 and 5 are irregular, but the verb *peeps* in line 4, with its accent and plosive sound, clearly gets the number-one slot. The repetition of *hold, hold* in line 5 speaks powerfully for itself. You'll also notice that trying to scan lines 4 and 5 can be messy work because of their irregular rhythm. On the other hand, the irregularity gives a nice musical variety to the language and keeps the section of dialogue from becoming unnaturally rhythmic or boring. Shakespeare uses iambs because of the fact that it sounds very close to the way normal English is structured rhythmically. Therefore, when he chooses to break his established rhythm it still sounds right, while providing necessary variation that draws in the ear rather than rhythmically lulling the listener to sleep—as childhood verses like "Twinkle, Twinkle" sometimes do.

At the top of the scene, Lady Macbeth is reading her husband's letter, a letter that is written in prose. You might not have noticed this, and if you did, it was probably because of how the prose looks on the page rather than because of the sound. It blends with the language that follows, proof again that the difference between spoken normal English and patterned verse is a subtle one. Shakespeare often goes from verse to prose and back again. The reasons for the playwright introducing this variation would make a good topic for discussion, but I won't take that up here. I'll simply tempt you with a question. Why does Shakespeare do so?

When I studied Shakespeare in college as an English major, and later as an MFA graduate student in acting, my teachers would hammer the importance of scansion. I think they overemphasized its place. No one wants to listen to Shakespeare that sounds overly rhythmic, and the best professional actors wouldn't even consider tying themselves rigidly to scansion. Good actors make the language sound as natural as poetic language can possibly sound, at the same time using the language's imagery to make dramatic points. Nevertheless, scansion is a valuable investigative tool for finding the words that get the meaning across. But scansion should not be the absolute arbiter of how a line should be read. As that colleague from the English Department always reminds me, "The important part of scansion is that it helps you find the five accented syllables per line. Find them, and find the heart of the meaning of the line."

IDEA UNITS

Another effective way of determining how to read a line comes from dividing up a passage into idea units or phrases, and determining which of those carry the most meaning. Let's take a look.

> The raven himself   is hoarse
> That croaks   the fatal entrance   of Duncan
> Under my battlements.   Come, you spirits
> That tend   on mortal thoughts,   unsex me here,
> And fill me   from the crown   to the toe top-full
> Of direst cruelty.   Make thick   my blood,
> Stop up   th' access and passage   to remorse,
> That no   compunctious visitings   of nature
> Shake   my fell purpose,   nor keep peace   between
>   Th' effect   and it.   Come   to my woman's breasts,
> And take my milk   for gall,   you murd'ring ministers,
> Wherever   in your sightless substances
> You wait   on nature's mischief.

By separating each line or sentence into the individual idea units they contain, you will begin to be able to see the power of each phrase. This understanding will give you an opportunity to work with the colors and specific picture each idea unit possesses. Breaking the dialogue into its stresses through scansion is effective for finding and delivering the clarity of the line, but having pictures of the idea units as you read will help you convey a more nuanced meaning—because you will be generating specific images as you read aloud—through the pictures you hold in your head and then convey.

Dividing each line into phrases as we have done here does not ultimately mean that you should be taking pauses (or finding caesuras) in the line when you read a passage aloud. That is what the punctuation is for. However, if you take the time to separate the lines into their individual units, you will be able to explore those images and how the images work in connection with each other. As you become familiar with what each phrase contains, you will become more proficient at painting the phrase images aloud without taking unnecessary pause time.

At this point, you might want to try saying aloud some of the colorful phrases from the passage beginning with "the raven." Try repeating the phrases until you can convey a specific picture. Then put some of them together. You will hear some very chilling readings with these images. Notice, for instance, the power of the K and M sounds in connection with the blood image in "Make thick my blood." Or the soft M–M sound of "my milk" when set against the hard contrasting G sound in the phrase that follows—"for gall."

ALLITERATION

Alliteration, or repetition of consonant sounds, is another method for helping to find the words that are most important to stress in a line of Shakespeare. The term has already been mentioned several times in our discussion. The amount of alliteration found in Shakespeare makes it clear that the bard loved to use it and thought it to be an effective device for drawing attention to the images he painted in a basic and visceral way. His ability to use alliterative sounds in conjunction with the specific meaning of a line and the dramatic feel going on at a particular moment is truly remarkable. By simply giving a nod to those repetitions vocally when they appear, you will possess another effective way to make the drama contained in the lines pop out in your spoken work.

You might want to return to the scene and underline the alliterations you find there. Try to figure out why Shakespeare might have used alliteration when and where he does, as I did a few paragraphs ago in the discussion of phrasing. Then try reading aloud those alliterative passages from the scene, emphasizing the alliterative sounds. You will be amazed at the power the repetitive sound can have dramatically. Keep in mind that the sound of English has changed in the last four hundred years and a phrase like "my keen knife," which is no longer alliterative, would have been so back then. Certainly the repetition of the hard K sound would effectively draw attention to the strength of intent that Lady Macbeth demonstrates here.

Spending time going through this process will no doubt make you a more skilled reader, which in turn will make the time spent on learning your lines and applying them vastly more effective. But perhaps more important is the fact that if you go through this process, you will be discovering for yourself experientially how the language of Shakespeare is both incredibly powerful and beautiful. This has to lead to a more effective approach toward acting this type of material.

APPOSITION AND ANTITHESIS

We began our discussion of analysis of the language with the topic of punctuation—the traffic signs for the eye when reading Shakespeare. But an actor also must provide some traffic signs for the ear—if the listening audience is to comprehend the throughline of action and get at the level of complexity that a Shakespearean character possesses. The traffic signals we will focus on here are *antithesis* and *apposition,* and the use of transitions. We'll begin with antithesis and apposition.

Apposition is a term that comes from the same root as *opposite.* It refers to ideas that are set against each other in opposition. *Antithesis* is a related term that refers to words and phrases of opposite meaning that are purposely placed in contrast to each other in a line or sentence and that balance each other when the two ideas come together to form a complete whole. Here is an example to make what I am saying easier to grasp:

> Thy letters have transported me beyond
> This ignorant present, and I feel now
> The future in the instant.

In this example, *present* is contrasted against *future,* and by emphasizing these two words in apposition, the reader can get a lot mileage vocally from the contrast. Here is another, better example:

> To beguile the time,
> Look like the time; bear welcome in your eye,
> Your hand, your tongue; look like the innocent flower,
> But be the serpent under 't.<

This passage contains two sets of images in apposition. *Beguiling,* or fooling the time, is very different than looking like or blending with the time.

Contrasting the antithetical words when reading aloud produces clarity and ear-catching dramatic effect. The phrases *innocent flower* and *serpent under't* work in the same way. Recognizing and using such contrasts can turn a flat, black-and-white reading into a 3D experience. Once you grasp the concept, you can take a look at the ideas in apposition in Lady Macbeth's speech where she categorizes her husband's strengths and weakness as a potential murderer. It is loaded with antithetical ideas.

Antithesis offers up another skills-building opportunity for the detective in you, regardless of the Shakespearean play you are working on.

FINDING AND USING TRANSITIONS

Just one more term before we leave the subject of Shakespeare's language. The word is *transition,* and it refers to the concept used by actors to describe the moment you shift from one idea to another. A transition to a new subject invariably causes a change of tone, a shift in color, a different use of energy, or a new purpose in what your character is saying. When you recognize where these shifts occur, you can make an adjustment in the reading that will keep the listener's ear from being lulled to sleep and will keep your character multileveled and interesting. Let's go back now to Lady Macbeth's first speech after reading the letter from her husband. Find that speech earlier in the chapter and mark with a double slash each of the places where you think transitions occur in the speech. Then check your choices against mine, which follow here. Don't read on until you have done your own work.

The raven himself is hoarse
That croaks the fatal entrance of Duncan
Under my battlements. // Come, you spirits
That tend on mortal thoughts, unsex me here,
And fill me from the crown to the toe top-full
Of direst cruelty. // Make thick my blood,

Stop up th' access and passage to remorse,
That no compunctious visitings of nature
Shake my fell purpose, nor keep peace between
Th' effect and it. // Come to my woman's breasts,
And take my milk for gall, you murd'ring ministers,

Wherever in your sightless substances
You wait on nature's mischief. // Come, thick night,
And pall thee in the dunnest smoke of hell,
That my keen knife see not the wound it makes,
Nor heaven peep through the blanket of the dark
To cry "Hold, hold!"

[*Enter* MACBETH]

// Great Glamis, worthy Cawdor,
Greater than both by the all-hail hereafter,
Thy letters have transported me beyond
This ignorant present, and I feel now
The future in the instant.

Now compare your markings with my own. In the first section, Lady M makes a declaration about the future. In the second section, she begins to call on the spirits and makes an initial but general call for their help in converting herself to evil. Next she makes a specific list of things they can do to her to strengthen her resolve. Then she actually asks to be changed from her natural womanly nature. Next she asks for the protection of darkness to shield her from failure. Finally, in the biggest transition of all, she changes tone and style completely to properly greet her husband. In your own analysis, you might have lumped Lady Macbeth's wish list together as one long playable action. That's fine, too. But either way, in a list like this one there is a logical progression that must build vocally—if the reading is to escalate dramatically. With a little practice, you will be able to handle all of this.

CONCLUSION

An understanding of the dramatic situation of a scene, when combined with a close study of how the words operate together, will enable you to truly make Shakespeare come alive. With a little determination on your part, you can and will learn to read some of the greatest words in the English language in a way that does them justice—as a product from not only our greatest poet, but our greatest dramatist.

We have covered a lot of ground in this chapter. Perhaps the descriptions and examples of the reading tools listed were too limited to give you enough confidence to plunge ahead. If you need a more detailed set of descriptions and a larger assortment of examples, there are many excellent, inexpensive books you can go to. *Clues to Acting Shakespeare* by Wesley Van Tassel, published by Allworth Press, is outstanding. It will provide you with all the answers and examples you'll need. His book was a great help in my own preparation of this chapter. *(exuent)*

CHAPTER

SEVEN

STYLE—FINDING THE WORLD OF THE PLAY

THE ARTISTIC AND COMMERCIAL SUCCESS OF ROB Marshall's film *Chicago* a few years ago spurred a mini-resurrection of the movie musical. For years there had been talk of trying to bring the seemingly moribund genre back to the screen. Producers with a vision and a pocketful of money had long been imagining what a filmed version of *Les Mis* or another Broadway classic might look like. But it was *Chicago*'s success that really made it happen. How long the resurrection will last probably depends on the success of the spate of recent releases—*The Phantom of the Opera, Rent,* and *The Producers*—and the more recent indicators haven't been good.

Was *Chicago*'s success an anomaly, or have the crop of filmed musicals failed with audiences because they have failed to find a successful stylistic translation from stage to screen? And the issue of *style* will be at the heart of this chapter. Although at first glance style seems more a matter for a director to be concerned with, your choices as an actor are ultimately formed by the world of the play in which you find yourself. Your contributions regarding that world can help make or break both the story you help tell and the character you are charged with bringing to life.

The term *style* is a concept not easily made tangible for discussion. Like the concepts of art or beauty in some college aesthetics course, *style* is difficult to define and even more difficult to agree about. In preparation for this chapter, I looked through well over a dozen books on theatre—from the intro books to books on directing. The intro books made no mention of the concept, and the directing books tap-danced their way through the subject, admitting that style is a dicey thing to talk about. The best discussions I found were in the script analysis books, and even there, the term *style* was often, by the authors' own admission, treated in a loosey-goosey manner. One of the best definitions I found was in *Script Analysis* by David Grote, a terrific book, by the way. He says that style is "*the manner in which all the elements of the play are integrated into a single whole*" (my italics). That definition works perfectly for me, because it is exactly what I will be talking about here.

In my opinion, style in production can be *a* critical, if not *the* critical, ingredient of a production, and Marshall's film of *Chicago* bears this out. For that reason, I think it is essential that the term be one that is tackled in an acting book that puts so much focus on analysis. But before we proceed, let me try a bit harder to objectify the term *style* more fully. It's the least I can do—if I am going to expect you to start thinking in stylistic terms and ultimately make it a part of your analysis process.

Style is the concept shared by the artists who collaboratively design a production and those who enact it. Every director and production team searches for a style that will bring their project to life before setting sail on their journey toward production. Theatre people know that a production's success or failure often depends on finding just the right manner in which to present all the elements of their story. For that reason, *style* is a term that you really must get into your active vocabulary.

The agreed-upon style for any production is like its map or compass. A successfully conceived and executed style can indicate the route for a successful journey. It can prevent a production from wandering on the high seas or foundering on the shoals. A stylistic miscalculation can have the opposite effect and hurl a production off course or onto the rocks. *Style,* then, to build on Grote's definition, might be defined as the manner in which a production team chooses to bring a script to life. It is a shared vision that all elements of a production must fit into—from the set and lights to the acting on the stage. But a more practical way of understanding style might be to think of it as the created "world of the play." This agreed-upon vision is intended to serve the script that inspired it by making that script work effectively for an audience that watches. A successful production style is always consistent and helps make the story clear, accessible, compelling, and meaningful. An ineffective style can leave an audience saying, Huh?" or worse, "Yeah, so what?"

All right, in an effort to further define and develop our concept of style, let's try to apply our understanding of the term to the spate of musical films that have been released recently. At this writing, *The Producers, Rent, The Phantom of the Opera,* and *Chicago* have all come and gone and are available on DVD. It would be a great idea to view any or all of these films in conjunction with reading this chapter. It will help make any shortcomings in my discussion of style more apparent. It will also let you know how and where my own critical and analytical perceptions about these musicals differ from your own.

Generally, musicals are not my favorite theatrical form. Yes, I enjoy them when they are well done, and yes, I have performed in them and directed them, but more often than not I find them lacking in substance and depth (shows like *Sweeney Todd* and *Sundays in the Park with George* excepted). In short, I usually prefer spending my theatrical time elsewhere. But even when it comes to the light stuff, the manner in which it's done (its style) is able to trump its lack of substance.

For his filmed production, Rob Marshall found a way to brilliantly translate *Chicago*'s unusual but clearly theatrical material for the screen. He molded an ideal storytelling style for the piece. Originally developed for and with Bob Fosse's particular skills and personal style for the stage, the movie version of *Chicago,* while retaining the spirit of the source material, became something new and original—a state-of-the-art tour de force for the screen. Onstage, *Chicago* possesses a kinetic and muscular score and script perfectly suited for the Fosse style. Marshall, a brilliant theatrical director and choreographer in his own right, through his use of quick cutting and music-video angles and editing, enhanced the kinetic feel while keeping the thin story moving clearly yet frantically forward toward climax and resolution. The net result felt like a 1930s newsreel updated and on speed. The world the film's characters moved in was fast, harsh, and unrelenting. It all worked perfectly, taking its contemporary audience on a breathtaking and thrilling ride where story, character, theme, music, dance, and Marshall's own fabulous creative imagination worked together as an aesthetic whole. Both critics and ticket buyers responded positively to the amalgam.

Though *Chicago*'s filmic style seems apparent to me, the untrained eye might take its look and feel for granted and assume that Marshall's final product is the natural fulfillment of the written script. But those of us who have directed realize that a script is merely the blueprint for what ultimately gets onstage or onscreen. And the journey from page to stage is often a bumpy one. And though style might be taken for granted by some and not ever be thought about by others, it often spells the difference between success and failure. To varying degrees, the film versions of *Phantom, Rent,* and *The Producers* reflect this fact.

The movie version of *The Phantom of the Opera,* one of the most successful theatrical musicals of all time, produced the box office reaction I mentioned earlier—the crushing "Yeah, so what?" The critical reaction was even harsher. In fairness to the film version, the stage version of *Phantom* never knocked critics over, either. Turgid, with cardboard characters and a musical score that was florid but forgettable, *Phantom's* biggest claim to fame was its spectacle—from opera house to sewer—, which climaxed in that legendary chandelier episode. So how does that emphasis on spectacle translate to a successful film? Obviously, the movie's producers including the show's savvy composer, Andrew Lloyd Webber, thought the answer lay in getting that spectacle across to its audience in movie terms. No doubt that's why Joel Schumacher was hired for the job. The former artist who once designed window displays for department stores, and who directed and created the atmospherics for the first films in the *Batman* franchise, seemed the perfect stylist for the job. But the pictures Schumacher made for *Phantom,* opulence notwithstanding, were dull and static. And so were the film's plot and two-dimensional characters. Even the charms of Emmy Rossum and the skills of Patrick Wilson were unable to breathe life into his *Phantom,* and Gerard Butler's portrayal of the phantom was creepy and without charm. He could not make us like him, nor care about him, which doesn't leave an audience much to root for. The acting style in general meandered from stiff (Butler) to over-the-top (Minnie Driver as the diva). Schumacher has never been accused of good storytelling, and the world he created could not come close to holding us. The film tanked at the box office after being drubbed by the critics. It had not found a stylistic glue to hold it together and make it work.

Rent, another theatrical blockbuster, one with an incredibly loyal youth-based cult following, headed straight down the failure road, as well. In the rousing opening number, director Chris Columbus paid homage to the original theatrical version by filming the characters singing on an actual stage, much like in the original. The film then segued into a setting in the realistic streets of New York and quickly went downhill. There was plenty of cold-air breath smoke to remind us that winter in New York can be harsh on bohemians. But little else besides the look of the film was likely to be confused with reality, making this stylistic choice a kiss of death. The screenplay offered up more character dialogue than the stage version (which had almost none and played like an opera), but the dialogue was cliché-ridden and driven by the goal of pushing the action forward rather than by any organic needs of its characters. The support-group dialogue was particularly awful, and Columbus helped remind us of the fact by dwelling continuously in close-ups. The cast, many from the original stage production, though looking too old, were sincere and likable. But having the camera up their noses for all the emotional moments only drew attention to the fact that the dialogue was rank and the songs didn't come naturally or easily out of it. Details that reminded us this "just ain't real" kept compromising the stark reality Columbus seemed to be going for, and the plot contrivances could be seen from miles away. Mark the genius filmmaker, for instance, didn't know how to hold a camera, and he treated it like a video recorder when he's supposed to be shooting film. The stage version seduced us into taking the ride, and we didn't have time to see all of the play's shortcomings, at least while we were watching. Again, the stylistic choices emphasized *Rent*'s weaknesses rather than helping it work.

The Producers opened to mixed reviews and did disappointing business in spite of heavy advertising and lots of promotion by its stars, Nathan Lane and Matthew Broderick. Of the new filmed musicals, only *The Producers* seemed to have found a filmic style that actually helped make it work, and in this case, it was because director Susan Stroman (who directed the stage version, as well) had the sense to keep what worked on the stage for the film. In fact, the movie version of *The Producers* seemed, for the most part, like watching the stage play. Stroman kept her static cameras in front of the performing actors and let them do most of the work. There was little attempt to radically change what worked for the stage. Though hardly to be confused with art, at least *The Producers* managed to be entertaining—that is, if you find Mel Brooks entertaining.

Even if you've never directed a movie musical, you know the difficulty of bringing a script from page to stage if you have ever had to direct a scene for class, or even worked on one as an actor. You know from experience that finding the way to deliver and execute material is not only a directing problem. As an actor, you face the same problem every time you pick up a script. Your ability to find an acting style that works with the material you are working on is an issue you face when you embark on a new scene. Even the term *realism* as it relates to an individual script varies in accordance with that material.

Here is an example of what I mean. In its day, any play by Clifford Odets was considered the epitome of realism. But open the pages of his *Awake and Sing!* today and you will have a hard time hearing the dialogue found there consistent with your idea of realism. In the same way, were you to watch at a gangster movie from the 1930s, you would find it hard to believe that eighty years ago, critics and movie watchers considered what looks today like an over-the-top style as anything approaching realistic. Nevertheless, were you to do a scene from *Awake and Sing!* or, for that matter, *Dead End,* you would need to find a way to deliver the goods believably and effectively to the audience.

Believable, of course, is not synonymous with *realistic. Believability* refers to believable for the world the play. A contemporary realistic delivery of Shakespeare's dialogue would make the language dull and probably unclear. As you learned in the previous chapter, a Shakespearean production's success will be invariably be linked with the ability to make the language interesting and accessible to the listening audience. The acting style will be heightened somewhat in accordance with the language. Believability in a farce is also not synonymous with realism. Though contemporary farces start out realistically, the characters in a farce are forced to go well beyond what many of us might consider realistic behavior. Nonetheless, actors playing such parts must make the audience believe that their characters would do so, resulting in a style of acting that we might say is realistic and beyond. But if the farce is to work, its actors must carry out actions with energy and commitment that in real life might be reserved only for the insane.

Musicals also require a sense of what will work and what will not in order to bring the material to life. Ultimately, the good musical theatre actor understands this and is able to adjust his or her performance choices and execution accordingly. An actor performing in *Dames at Sea* cannot be operating in the same manner as when performing in *Sweeney Todd* or, for that matter, *Carousel* or *Oklahoma!* And *The Music Man* requires a far different set of wheels than does *My Fair Lady* or *Bat Boy.* So how do you learn to do this?

One of the most important ways that we learn is by trial and error. Every time you begin your voyage from selection of a play to its opening night or its presentation in class, you learn and get better through your experience. And during the course of your training and career, you will be able to chart your growth. But if you're planning on a professional career, you will have only a limited time to learn all you need to know before you will be out there pounding the pavement trying to find work to pay your rent. You need to learn all you can now while you're in class and while you're working on productions. But you can also learn a great deal from a careful viewing of movie musicals or videos of stage productions—if you know how to watch them.

Watching videos of productions may be something you already do, but doing so with an eye toward what works, what doesn't, and why can be an effective addition to what you learn on your feet by trial and error.

What follows is a hopefully challenging set of questions that can go a long way toward getting you to think actively about the choices others have made, and toward getting you to be proactive about your own thinking and, ultimately, your own work.

Next time you're watching a DVD, consider these questions:

> Did you like this play? Why or why not? Can you separate the play itself from the production of the play? Would different choices in putting the play together change your opinion about the play? Did you like the production and not the play? What causes you to think this way?
>
> Did the play work? What is the definition of *work* as it is used in this context? What is required to make the play work? How can this be done?
>
> What is the genre of the play? Were the production choices consistent with the genre? Did those choices help make the play work? Explain. What is the style of the production? How does it serve to make the play work? Fail to do so?
>
> What is the balance of entertaining versus enlightening in this play? How do they work together in the production? Did the production find the appropriate balance? Explain.
>
> What do you think was the playwright's intention in writing this play? Was it supported by the production? Explain. How might the playwright's intention be better supported?

What is the spine or major idea behind the play? How is it brought out in the film? If not brought out adequately, how could it be done better? Is it necessary that a major idea be communicated to the audience? Is it more important in some musicals than others? Why? How important is it to this musical? Why or why isn't it important?

What is the central conflict of the play? Is the conflict the engine of drama in the play? Are there other elements that hold your interest more than the action? Why? Were these other elements brought out effectively? How so?

Which of Aristotle's elements of drama (action, character, dialogue, spectacle, music, idea) is/are the most important in this play, and why? Do the production choices serve to bring out the most important element or elements? How does it do so or fail to do so? What might have been done to improve the production in terms of these elements?

Do the production elements work together stylistically to create a consistent world of the play? Why or why not? Explain.

Who is/are the protagonist/s and antagonist/s of this play? Why? Why is knowing this fact important to production choices? Did the production make good use of the adversarial relationship? Relate your answer to the mechanics that make the play work.

Discuss the acting of the production. What is its relation to the overall effectiveness of the production?

Discuss the elements in this production other than acting that contribute to its success or failure. Discuss how the various elements integrate and serve each other and the overall whole.

Discuss the direction of the production.

Discuss physical action in the play and how it is used to tell the story. What specific things would you do in a production to make this play work effectively?

How effective was the casting in this production? Explain. If the style of the production were different, would your casting choices still be the same? Explain your answer. Cast this play yourself and justify your casting by using the script and stylistic choices for support.

What were the most effective moments in this play or production, and why?

Evaluate the scenic, lighting, and costume choices made for this production and how they work together to create the world of the play. Describe and justify the scenic, lighting, and costume choices you would make if directing a production of this play.

Before closing, just two more notes on style.

Just the mention of *Oklahoma!* has always sent nasty shivers down my back. I first saw it as a kid in summer stock. I thought it was dull and purposeless, except for the tunes, which have been so overplayed in my head that the charm has long ago abandoned ship. *Oklahoma!* for me, in other words, had nothing going for it except its value as a historical document. The film version did nothing to change my mind–it offered a mélange of styles mixing cinemascope outdoor vistas with stagey theatrical sets that self-consciously proclaimed, "I am a movie; no, I'm a stage play." For these reasons, I have avoided any contact with *Oklahoma!* since childhood. But in preparation for writing this chapter, I watched the recent and highly praised Trevor Nunn production starring Hugh Jackman that was broadcast on PBS. Because of its beautiful integration of stylistic elements—from set and lighting, to casting, to acting, to staging—for the first time I got *Oklahoma!* I found that it *is* beautiful, and charming, and that its simplicity is an asset, not a stodgy manifestation of its outdatedness. Trevor Nunn's direction wielded a magic wand that changed a pumpkin into a magnificent coach for me. I would like to apologize publicly to Mr. Rodgers and Mr. Hammerstein.

Finally, in as few words as possible. I recently watched a highly praised box office sensation, that Chinese movie with the crazy name, *Kung Fu Hustle.* It's ridiculous and fabulous—somewhere between an old Bruce Lee film and Busby Berkeley. It is a live-action Looney Tune, one in which Bugs and the gang start dancing when the urge strikes. It works because director Stephen Chow invents a style for the film that makes it work. I can't think of a film that better demonstrates the power of style or the need to create and maintain the world of the play. Any Pixar film, feature-length or short subject, accomplishes the same kind of magic. See them, study them, marvel at them. Any of the films mentioned in this paragraph will make the concept of style seem self-evident.

PART 2
ONGOING AND LONG-TERM THINGS

CHAPTER EIGHT

MAKING YOURSELF DIRECTOR-PROOF

ONE OF THE MOST IMPORTANT LESSONS I LEARNED AS A professional actor is that it's the actor's responsibility—not the director's—to build your performance. I tell my BFA acting students this all the time, and it's something you'd better learn quickly.

"Ninety percent of the directors you work with won't help you," I tell them.

"You're on your own, pal. You better figure out what you're doing!" And, "You've gotta learn how to act on your own to protect yourself from all the bad directors you're gonna work for." And, "You better bring in something good, or you're gonna die up there."

My students, of course, think I'm deeply cynical. That's understandable, because these takes on the actor–director relationship in the professional theatre are nothing like what they've experienced while working on productions in college. The fact is the professional theatre is different from college and high school, as I was reminded recently when I performed in a regional theatre production for the first time in a long while.

There are fundamentally three possible approaches that directors take to working with actors:

1. The director tells the actors exactly what he wants them to do.
2. The director helps lead the actors to desirable choices while making it seem like the actors are making these choices themselves.
3. The director offers the actors very little regarding what they are doing, one way or another.

In high schools and colleges, most directors fall into one of the first two categories, and the resulting product more often than not makes the actor look and feel good and works for the play overall. In my professional experience, however, fewer directors than you might think use either of these approaches, and even those who do don't necessarily produce a happy or successful outcome. For one thing, most professional actors would balk at a type 1 director who micromanages them. A type 2 director and an actor might make a happy marriage on a professional production—if the actor and director are on the same page, and if there's time in the abbreviated rehearsal period (typically three weeks for an Equity regional theatre production) for them to do the time-consuming work of discovering the role together.

But more often than not, a director in the professional theatre stays away from the actor's process. The director may talk about results or what she wants to see, but rarely will she give actors much help on how to get there. The actor is often left to his or her own devices until the show opens—or until the director explodes because what is happening onstage is not working and the director feels obliged to do something about it. Of course there are many wonderful directors, but I'm generalizing here to make a point, and the point is: for every director who will work patiently with actors to explore their roles, there are many who can't be bothered, or who expect actors to take care of their own business.

That is why you must develop your acting craft so that you can work independently. You must be able to find, on your own, the way to tell the story of the play through what your character says and does. If you are a student at the high school or college level, you might want to ask yourself a question or two about your goals in acting class or in the rehearsal studio. What do you want get from doing a production or, for that matter, from your time in acting class? If it's just the glory and fun of performance, you might be missing a great opportunity for developing the craft you will need in the future. Here are a couple more questions for consideration. When you are being directed in a production, is your director concerned with what you are learning, or just getting up the show? Is she more interested in teaching you something, or in making you look good? If you're not learning much from your director, you might want to reconsider the way you go through your own rehearsal process and begin trying on your own to solve the problems of the play, of each scene, and of your character.

When a math teacher gives you an answer to a problem, that probably means she wants to see your work, the *how* of how you got there. You should consider your rehearsal obligations in the same way. You need to be able to go through the process correctly and on your own and come up with the solution. Only when you can do this will you be ready to work in the profession—because you will have the acting craft you will need to sustain you. So you may not want to settle for putting something up in the future without having made the effort to analyze it, plan it out, and rehearse it with as much commitment as you can carry. A director's fix may help you look good, but it won't necessarily make you the independent artist an actor should be.

I consider myself a teaching director. When I begin a production, I try to lay out for my actors in general terms the story we're going to be telling an audience, and what I need for each of my actors to provide. I give them enough in a general sense so they'll be able to make choices independently within the overall framework I've set up. In other words, I have provided a structure that we all hope and expect will allow my students the chance to make choices independently but within parameters that I have already defined for them. Thanks to this structure, even when students come up with choices that I don't think will best serve the production, their work is usually salvageable, because they're never that far afield. As a result, my students seldom feel like they have failed, and their willingness to use their imagination, instincts, and intelligence is seldom compromised. Most importantly, they are learning to think and work independently as actors.

When actors talk about an "actor's director" on interview shows like *Inside the Actors Studio,* they usually mean a director who has helped them make choices and shape their work in an effective way. Whenever they talk about this kind of director, they seem to light up. The reality is that many directors, especially in film, have not been trained to do that. Even many stage directors do not have the eye or the vocabulary to get what they want from an actor, although most of them think they do. Worse, many directors are perfectly able to recognize when something is not working but can't define the problem or articulate a way to fix it. When that is the case, the actor had better be ready to step in and take care of business herself. Because when the director is treading water or drowning, it does not relieve the actor from the responsibility of producing a successful performance.

I've been saying this kind of stuff for years, using for the most part my memories of my own experiences in the profession, or my observations of directors other than myself working with their actors in rehearsals, mostly here at my school. But not too long ago, after a fourteen-year hiatus, I returned to the professional stage to update my opinions, refill my empathy tank for dealing with my own students and their problems, and see whether I have learned anything about my own acting. Here's what happened.

The play was *White People* by J. T. Rogers, discussed previously. As you may recall, the play is an examination of attitudes about race that was being produced at a local regional theatre. There were to be two weeks of rehearsal including run-throughs and all dress rehearsals, and five weeks of performances. Bottom line—very short rehearsal, nice run.

The play consists of interlocking monologues by three characters. The rehearsals, for the most part, were divided among the three actors in the play, who rehearsed individually onstage without any interaction until we did run-throughs only a few days later. Since each actor was responsible for about thirty-five minutes of monologue and there was so little time for actual rehearsal, I worked intensely on my own before rehearsals began. By the time of the first formal rehearsal, I had my part memorized and had already made initial choices about the interpretation of the words, my character, and the physical actions my character would make. Since there was so little time during actual rehearsals for any kind of exploration, I wanted to get as much as possible done before our first meeting. I needed, of course, to accommodate all of my choices to the set and make the necessary adjustments required by my director. Ultimately, we all wanted our work to serve the playwright and have the desired effect on the audience.

I came to the first rehearsal extremely nervous. I had been that way for weeks, worried that I would not be up to the job. Therefore, it was imperative to me that I come in totally memorized. I had no idea how much my nerves would compromise me, so I wanted to be a hundred percent off book when I arrived. I was already anticipating the first read-through, wondering whether I should try to do it from memory. If I attempted to go from memory and I nerved out, how would that set me back? On the other hand, if I simply read, I would only be postponing the maiden voyage without book. I tabled the question as the formal first rehearsal began.

After the introductions were made, the contracts signed, and the Equity deputy elected, the set designer presented his renderings, which is a common occurrence at first rehearsals. I was expecting to see a desk, the central item in my imaginary set—the one I had made my preliminary blocking and acting choices with. My part of the play took place in a law office high above downtown St. Louis overlooking the Mississippi River. Though not stated directly, this is all clearly implied in the script. What would be the most prominent feature of a lawyer's office? A desk. The designer had apparently not read too carefully, however, and had not been sure whether my character's action took place in a law office or some other business setting, nor whether he was in his home or at the offices of the firm.

The director, though obviously clear on the play, was fuzzy on some of the details, having just come off a previous directing job. He was still catching up and since he had worked with this designer before, had apparently allowed him free rein. He was happy there wasn't a desk, because the stage was small and a desk would take up a lot of space. I wasn't. Much of what I had worked out for my character was based on the assumption, a good one, I think, that the set would have a desk. I was upset that I was going to have to rethink so much of my physical action.

As we went through the first reading, it became clear to everyone that my character's setting was indeed his office, but since there was so little space to work with, the director wanted to go without the desk on the set. I was to imagine there was a desk somewhere just out of reach of the actual playing area. I was to imagine that I had moved my chair away from the desk because I was using it near my bookshelves while I packed up my office. At least we agreed that packing was one of the pieces of business I could wrap my monologues around.

I ended up doing some of the first read-through without referring to the script, by the way, but like a beginning cyclist, I never let my hands get too far from the handlebars. I was nervous, but I got into it at spots, and no one seemed to be laughing at me. I felt like I had made it over the first hurdle.

One of the biggest unknowns for me was how the audience needed to perceive my character in order for the ending of the play to be dramatically effective. I knew that my character was not particularly likable, but I thought that the audience needed to feel for me at the end of the play. I tried in my own rehearsals to find a balance that would be true to the character but still give the audience enough to empathize with me eventually. I also knew I needed a director's eye to look at my work from an audience's perspective—something most actors cannot do completely on their own.

The abbreviated rehearsal period flew by, and since I actually got only a third of the overall time allotted, the reality was that I didn't rehearse all that much. A good chunk of the time we did have was spent in staging the play, not analyzing, experimenting, or developing. So what I brought in was not so different from what I would show an audience on opening night. In some ways I was very disappointed in the process, in others absolutely satisfied. Let me explain.

It has been said more than once that casting is 80 percent of the director's responsibility. This axiom held true in the production I was part of. My two colleagues were very well cast, and I could see, even during our first read, that they well suited the roles they would be playing. They probably would have said the same about me. As a matter of fact, I had always admired our director's ability to cast. Having seen many of his productions in the past—many as a critic, by the way—I had always been impressed with how he matched actor with role. A director with good casting instincts finds that something that the actor naturally has that will make a good conjunction with the role he is playing. My director obviously did that.

During our blocking rehearsal, I was expecting our director to start me off and have several specific things he wanted me to do at various parts of the play, especially in the "big moment" places. That was certainly how I proceeded when I was doing all my prerehearsal work. But that's not the way it unfolded. For the most part, he let me begin where I was comfortable, and I moved through my words and actions, fitting them into the little space I had on the set. More often than not it was I who stopped the flow, because of a line problem or because I did not execute an action the way I wanted to. Occasionally, he stopped to ask me about a choice or to refine something I had done, but seldom did he disagree or have a problem with what I was doing.

Often I moved through large sections of the script forgetting to write down any blocking. I was often expecting that he would stop me at any moment, and at times I was totally caught up in what I was doing. Although I was very nervous, the adrenaline rush was pushing me to do things that were surprising even to me, imaginative things that were often emotionally connected, and big. When I would realize after a while that I had not been keeping tabs on what I had been physically doing in the space, I would panic and stop the action to ask the stage manager for a review. She would always feed back to me the sequence of the most recent things she saw, having erased any previous movement. But there were times when the most recent things I had done were experimental and hadn't necessarily worked. The stage manager assumed that each new thing I did had become the official blocking.

No one else seemed to have a problem with sticking to what we had done the time before. I was always aware that in one week we would be doing this play for an audience, and the insecure part of me wanted to settle on an approved route for my acting. I also felt uncomfortable with this process of creating my own spontaneous blocking that I would repeatedly forget to write down and would not remember when we went back to it. At those times I felt like a student, and a not very promising one—a bumbler who had to keep asking for his blocking because he hadn't been responsibly professional about getting it down in his script.

Fortunately, the blocking I was coming up with, for the most part, differed only in detail from what I had done earlier on my own, so that even when it was executed in a different order or on a slightly different area of the stage, its purpose and what it revealed about my character's thoughts and feelings were consistent.

For the most part, the director kept telling me that he liked what I was doing and that I was such an "organic actor," something I have never considered myself to be, and something I certainly wasn't feeling as we went through the blocking portion of rehearsal. This section of rehearsal wasn't really just blocking, though, because my concerns were on all aspects of my work, not just the movement. So my work *was* organic in the sense that my movement choices were coming out of my character's needs, thoughts, and feelings of the moment. Much of what I was doing, however, was not organic, in that I had already made the rudiments of many of these choices in my own work before actual rehearsals began. I was either playing with them here or adapting those choices to the new environment. Of course, there were moments where new stuff did just appear. But I was afraid they would be lost if I wasn't better able to record them in my memory bank. Unfortunately, I wasn't relaxed enough to just say, "Let's slow up the process!" On the one hand, I was too insecure to assert myself that way. On the other, I was afraid if we did slow down the process, we would run out of time before we had to perform this baby.

Nevertheless, in some ways the rehearsal process worked for me very well. The director assumed that I had done my homework and made sure I knew that he liked what I was doing. His encouragement affected me in a positive way, and as we moved through our rehearsals together I began shedding the debilitating fear that I had been hiding. The more relaxed I became, the more I was able to produce believable, real, and surprising moments, simply because I was available to them. Before long, he was having me run through whole speeches at a time, and then sections, and then my whole part, uninterrupted. There were never more than a few notes for me, but the one thing I got consistently was to make sure that I was aggressive in my approach to the audience rather than laid-back. I knew the difference and had been intentionally trying to relax more in spots, to see how little I could push and still make it work. Every time I did, however, I would get a note about it. In that sense, I was getting the director as representative of the audience, and I was finding out how much or how little I needed to do. That was helpful.

My big concern about how I was coming off to the audience and whether my big climax would be appropriately affecting to them never came up in discussion. When I finally asked about it, the director basically said, we'll see after we get an audience response. I was not happy with that answer. I wanted him as representative for the audience to help me make adjustments now, not after my stuff fell flat. But his complacency calmed me a bit, and I rationalized that it was not an issue.

The next step in the process was running the three characters' parts together, separating the monologues once again into the chunks in which they were actually written. It had been good working on our entire parts as a continuous entity. It had allowed us to solidify our individual dramatic arcs point by point. We hoped we would be able to keep what we had learned when it all was reintegrated. As we quickly worked through our scene changes and pickups, each of us realized how hard it was going to be, to sit onstage through several minutes of someone else's monologue yet be able to pick up emotionally where we had been several minutes before when we last spoke. At the same time, we were now being asked to find things to do to fill our downtime onstage rather than freeze in our positions. This was a great challenge, particularly toward the latter stages of the play. All of us were trying to find our own ways to maintain the emotional levels we would need when we next were on, but at the same time we were now being forced to distract ourselves by having to come up with real business to engage in (but quiet, uninteresting business that wouldn't upstage the actor who was speaking), all the while listening to each other so we wouldn't miss our cues.

This was nerve-racking and difficult, but after a few tries in each section we were back on track with our individual speeches, as each of us continued to look for business and listen at the same time, all while keeping our emotional circumstances either turned up or available as needed. Each of us felt like jugglers adding balls before we were ready to do so. One ball at a time, we realized, and we could eventually juggle them all. So each time through, we focused on one aspect of what we ultimately needed to be able to do. By the end of rehearsal, each of us had found spots in each other's monologues that actually helped emotionally prep us for our own next time up at bat. We incorporated listening for those sections specifically, to charge us emotionally as we continued to refine our work.

Only after we were able to get smoothly through the whole play a few times did our director finally take on the role of audience representative. He had expected the play to run an hour and a half without intermission. It was running at an hour and fifty, too long, he felt, for an audience to sit through. He was upset because he felt this compromised the play and, I suspect, because he didn't completely know how to resolve the issue. As he went through his notes after one of our few run-throughs, he had a suggestion here and a suggestion there for the other two actors about tightening up their work to gain some time. He also asked each of us to consider where we needed absolutely to take a pause and to eliminate them wherever possible.

When he got to my notes, his face reddened a bit, and I could see that he was upset, even though a watching stranger might never have noticed, so gentlemanly was his demeanor. "I don't know how many times 'ah' is actually written in the script," he began, "but I counted thirty-seven 'ahs' in the first section of your last speech alone. This play has certain rhythms and tempos, and if we follow them we will actually be cutting time and helping your performance. I hope you can make that adjustment."

I was totally shocked by this note. First of all, there was no way I had said "ah" thirty-seven times in one little section. Besides, there was no way he was sitting there counting them. He just said that outrageous number because he was pissed. Now I was pissed, too, and a little hurt, not so much by the content of his remark, but rather by the fact that he had not shared this major note with me sooner. These "ahs" had become a part of my work. They had developed in part as a result of my own vocal habit when I am looking for the right word, and in part because I had made a connection between the struggle of finding the right word in general and the struggle to find words when emotionally bereft. The more these little vocal tics seemed to work for me internally, the more liberties I had been taking by adding them in.

No matter how much they may have given me, however, as soon as my director pointed out how much they slowed down the work and compromised the built-in rhythms the playwright had provided, I knew he was right. But why hadn't he told me sooner? They were now a part of my memorized work. They had become habituated. How could I get rid of them overnight, and how would eliminating them change the emotional bearing of my character? What was I supposed to do now? I felt as if that one note, like a torpedo, had destroyed my whole ship. I was going to have to start all over, even though there was no time left to do so. For a moment, in my despair, it didn't matter that my additions were compromising the overall production. All I could think about was the fact that he had not given me this note sooner.

I went home directly after rehearsal that day and pulled out my script. I *had* made an enormous number of additions; I was shocked by how many. I tried reading aloud the sections of the script where I had been the most guilty. When I read them as written, they flowed. Clearly the script was more powerful without all the little "ah" moments I had added. The playwright had given me a well-crafted score that when played as written would have the same emotional effect as a great piece of music. Why would I have wanted to destroy that? Of course, I hadn't wanted to. My reading of the character had evolved organically and with good intentions. Nevertheless, I had done exactly what I so often warn my own students against. I had neglected my script, and I had made my own work more important than serving the overall play.

That night I spent many hours learning to undo what I had been doing. I went through every speech many times, eliminating as many "ahs" as I possibly could. By the time I went to bed late that night, I had restored most of the integrity of the script as written. It had been hard work, but I was glad that the director had pointed out the error of my ways. I was glad to now be delivering the lines as written. Once I had restored the integrity of the script, it was actually more powerful, took up far less time, and was easier to do. I fell asleep that night to the mantra I so often chant to my own students: "It's in the script, stupid!"

The next day we were to have a dress run-through followed by notes and then, a few hours later, a preview with an audience. After the run-through, my fellow cast members congratulated me on the changes I had made. They were amazed that I had been able to eliminate so much of my unnecessary baggage and shared with me how concerned they had been for me, knowing what a blow our director's note must have been. The director pulled me aside a few moments later and thanked me simply and profoundly. I was proud of myself for keeping it together and for being able to make the adjustments necessary, as a professional must, simply, effectively, and without fanfare. And independently.

The point here is that I did so much of my work independently, and it was good work. Our director had not been at all atypical in his approach with us. He cast us well, he expected us to do good work, and we did. But he did ultimately have responsibility for the final product, and he stepped in when he absolutely had to. It was uncomfortable for me, but that was my problem, not the director's. His sensibilities, ninth inning notwithstanding, helped me be the best I could be even though he had expected me to be the one driving. And he certainly kept me from doing my own thing at the expense of the production overall.

The show opened the next night and was a huge success. The playwright, J. T. Rogers, spent opening weekend with us and saw the first five performances. He was very pleased with our work and said it was, overall, the best production he had so far seen (there had been about five up to that point). After each show, he gave us line notes. He knew his play by heart, not because he had seen the play so many times, but because he had said it aloud so many times as he was writing it. As he explained it, he had struggled over every word, every phrase, wanting everything he wrote to be just right. His line notes were helpful, by the way, because in every case, the way he had written it was superior to any accidental changes we might have made as a result of a performance slip-up or mistakes we had learned through repetition in rehearsal. I can only imagine what he would have thought had he seen and heard what I had done to his script while still in my "ah" phase.

We were warmly received by our audiences—even though the play was designed to make them squirm in their seats, and did—and by Miami-area critics. The actors were praised for their passion and power, and their director was praised for getting that from them. The director was also praised for having a solid grasp of the material and a terrific approach to it. The lesson here is that the director had done his job in spite of the fact that, for me as an actor, there were times when I wanted much more from him. But if we look at the results, he did what he needed to do.

The moral of this story, then, is the one I started with at the beginning of this book. As actors, you will have to learn to do what you do by yourself, alone, independently. The world of professional theatre and film expects it of you. The time for rehearsal is short and pressurized, and it may not focus on the things you want it to, or be conducted the way you think it should. The director may or may not be there for you in any given production.

It will be your responsibility as a professional to show up with the goods at that first rehearsal, ready to work. If you're going to be able to do that, you are going to have to master your craft now, while you're still at school, or in a safe place where you can fall on your butt without any permanent scarring. If you're smart, without any dramatic "ahs" to slow you down, you'll commit yourself to that task and get on with it.

CHAPTER NINE

MEMORIZATION

IMAGINE FOR A MOMENT LIVING IN A TIME OR A PLACE where writing had not yet been invented. A time and place where there was no video, no digital, where words and images were created and then disappeared with the moment—unless of course, the words and images were important enough to make the effort to remember them. Such a world existed, of course, long ago, before the invention of writing. Back then, stories and secrets, accumulated knowledge, and important cultural information all had to be memorized in order to avoid oblivion. Back then, if things were forgotten, they were lost forever. The future itself depended on storing and maintaining information through the use of memory.

In the days before writing, the ability to preserve ideas through memorization was essential to humans' very existence. Progress and the future depended upon it. Things that had to be remembered were passed down generation through generation orally. That meant that anything worth keeping alive needed to be kept in someone's head—from the directions to the bison herd that might have been a walk of many weeks away, to the ingredients of intricate healing potions necessary to save lives, to the history of the tribe's great ancestors, who if angered could bring great pain or if pleased bring great bounty. Children were selected from birth to become the living libraries for any tribe that was to survive.

These walking, talking encyclopedia acquired skills for remembering at the same time they began learning the accumulated knowledge and culture of their tribe. Since one person could become the receptacle for vast amounts of information, it was essential that they could master the job. Over generations, as the amount of information needed to be stored grew, so did the ability to memorize and retain this information quickly and efficiently. In fact, anyone who lived in these prewriting times probably possessed powers of memory that far surpassed those of us today. Need is an incredibly effective teacher. Today, it is hard for us to imagine that Homer Sr. could pass down orally the entire *Odyssey* to Homer Jr. and that Junior could look forward to passing on his stored and retained *Odyssey* to his own Homer III. And so on and so on until, mercifully, someone invented writing and wrote it all down instead.

In more recent times, memorization was still considered a valuable if not essential part of the educational process. Just a century ago, properly educated students were still being asked to memorize great tracts of their Latin studies. Poems and important historical and civic documents were memorized, as well, because it was believed that the skills involved in memorization were important to the development of the mind overall and to good thinking in particular. Even when I was growing up, people were still in the habit of memorizing phone numbers, birthdays, television schedules, and many other useful pieces of day-to-day information. It was considered a virtue to know important historical names, places, and dates, as well as the historical trends and movements containing them. I specifically remember having to memorize the Gettysburg Address, the Declaration of Independence, and the Preamble to the Constitution. I can still remember much of this material. Today, however, all this information is a touch away on the computer and seems hardly worth the effort to memorize it. I'm sure most of you reading this would agree.

Though memorization may no longer be valued as an educational tool, or necessary to survival on a day-to-day basis, it is still an essential, though seldom discussed, aspect of any actor's toolkit. There is no way around it, if you are going to be employable, you must be able to learn your lines accurately and in a timely manner. You must be able to reliably deliver them when called upon to do so. This is certainly true on the professional level, and it should be the case at all levels. Disciplined and committed actors know that their lines need to be learned long before that opening-night curtain rises and that by the time it does, those lines should be as second nature as breathing. By opening night, the best actors are focused on reacting to the moment, not thinking about whether their next set of lines will appear when needed, or the shape they'll be taking if and when the lines do show up.

I am sure you have had the feeling of being totally in the moment onstage. And a wonderful feeling that is. It is a magical experience where you are no longer thinking about what you are going to do or say. You don't have to; it's all there. You are so well rehearsed that all of your energy goes into listening and reacting—because you no longer need to think about any of that stuff that you worked on during your preparation and rehearsal process. When you are in this zone, you act spontaneously; your lines are nuanced, and they rise from the specifics generated in the moment. No longer do your lines sound canned or sung. Better, this state you're in also infects those you work with—because in effect you are taking them out of their habit, as well, and bringing them into the moment with you. Everyone is better because of it. And the best part is that all this is happening without compromising one iota what you have been asked to do by the director and by the script. Yet everything you do is just better, more real, and more compelling. This is the highest form of acting, and it can never happen if you haven't learned your lines properly, if you haven't absorbed them totally into your being.

But what if you're not so good at memorizing? What if it takes you forever to get those lines down? What if you're great once you know the lines, but it's just so painful and time-consuming getting to that place, and you're worth being indulged until you do? Well, the fact is you may be great, but in the profession, no one will ever know it if you can't handle your actor's homework. The expectation is that you'll know the lines when you need to have them down. If you're dyslexic, if you have a learning disability, if you are just sloooow, no one in the business cares. That is your problem, and one that you're responsible for, no matter what the reasons. It is your job to work it out. It's your job to have the goods when you're supposed to. Why? Because if you don't, someone else does.

Now, don't get me wrong. I'm totally sympathetic if you're a slow learner. I am, too. But as a director, if you can't give me what I need, there's someone else who can. Your inability is affecting others, as well as my game plan for bringing my play along. I don't want you slowing me down, distracting me and others, or forcing me to change my plan. The production is not about you. If you are currently in the habit of thinking you're worth the trouble, you will have a rude awakening later on. So start considering your memorization problem as your cross to bear and begin learning how to bear it.

When I did that play *White People,* I had to learn thirty-five to forty minutes' worth of monologue after years without exercising my memorization muscles, so I know how painful the process can be. Monologues, as I'm sure you're well aware, are far more difficult to learn than dialogue with other actors. When you're going back and forth, your memory can be jogged by the dialogue you're taking in; not so with monologues. You're on your own. To learn a piece well enough to deliver it to an audience night after night without a net is one scary proposition. Believe me, I am now very familiar with the feeling of being onstage in front of an audience and fearful of going blank—with no one else there with me who can toss me a line or a hint.

With that experience as a catalyst, I have spent quite a lot of time researching how people memorize. I have learned that there is great deal of disagreement on what works and what doesn't. These differences are no doubt caused by individual variations in how we learn. But there is also a lot of agreement about how certain techniques can, when employed, make even the hardest heads more pliable about learning and retaining the lines they are offered.

I, for instance, have tried almost everything to get lines into my head. I have tried getting up at the crack of dawn when my mind is fresh and undistracted. I have tried doing my lines before bed so I could sleep on them overnight. I have recorded my lines into a tape recorder and recited along with my recording until I could scream. I have recorded my lines with no expression, and I have recorded them while emoting. But the fact is that no matter what I do, it is a slow and unpleasant process for me. After fourteen years away from acting, and with a brain now belonging to a slightly more than ripe middle-aged person, my return to acting—and, with it, to the memorizing process—was enlightening, to say the least.

Memorization was even harder than I remembered it to be. I was out of shape, out of practice, and without youthful flexibility. I spent hours every day just trying to get my words down. But I did get better the more I did it. In part, my mental muscles were getting used to the exertion, but the improvement also came because as I worked I started making connections with the words I had to memorize beyond the simple rote mechanics, and that, for me, was crucial. What I am saying here is that, for me, memorization worked best when I was connecting it to the story I was telling as an actor, when I was able to give the memorization meaning.

The fact is, each of us has several kinds of memory. When we memorize, are we seeing the words as they are printed on the page in our minds, or are we hearing them in our heads? The answer to that question depends on who we are and how we retain. It could be one, it could be the other, or both. Besides visual and auditory memory, however, we also have our muscle memory, our sense memory, our kinetic memory, and probably several more kinds of memory that I am not even aware of. As I worked through my part, I discovered that the more kinds of memory I activated, the better and more efficient I got at learning my lines.

Many years ago, I discovered that when I began blocking a scene during a scene-study rehearsal, by the time I finished I knew most of my lines fairly well. I realized that this was because I somehow associated my lines with the movements I was making while saying them. My muscle memory and my kinetic memory (my memory of moving from place to place) were apparently reinforcing the retention of the words I was saying. The repetition of rehearsal, combined with the various memories I was using, began to produce effective results.

More recently, I rediscovered during my prerehearsal work that thought and emotional associations helped me retain particular sections of dialogue. For instance, if, as my character, I was picturing my son specifically when I talked about him, I retained that image as well as the lines I was supposed to say. The more specific the image, the easier my lines came. Soon I had created a son with an almost shaved head; he wore black, and he sneered at me all the time. I also allowed this sneer to produce a feeling in me. Usually, picturing his sneer made me angry and resentful. This, too, help me retain the lines of that section. Later, as I ran the lines of the section together, I actually got the picture or feeling first, and it then triggered me to remember the lines.

I also rediscovered that, for me, saying lines aloud from the beginning of the memorization process greatly improved both my ability to remember them and my ability to get them out of my mouth smoothly and efficiently. This seems perfectly logical to me. When the words are being said aloud, all of the muscles that will sooner or later be involved in the process are coming aboard sooner. My tongue and lips, my facial muscles and body are all learning their parts, and the body memory associated with word production is being called into play. In addition, I am hearing the words in my ears as well as in my mind. I have more machinery working at once to help get those lines scratched into my thick skull.

Some actors I spoke to fear the kinds of memorization processes I have just described. They say that making these kinds of associations and physical commitments while memorizing lines might make them memorize a particular thought and feeling too early in the game, and that saying a line in a particular way might become habituated. They worry that if their ideas were to change as rehearsals progressed, they would be unable to make adjustments. They think that if they were to memorize these kinds of associations and ways of delivery at the beginning of their rehearsal journey, they would find themselves stuck with these choices at the other end, because they would be unable to jettison them later. These actors felt that all their dialogue needed to be memorized without association of idea, sound, and/or emotion.

In response I can only say that has not been my experience. In fact, one of the touchstones of good acting, it seems to me, is the ability to adjust to the nuances of change that might occur at any time during a rehearsal process, or, for that matter, during a performance. The really good actor is able to show the flexibility necessary to adjust to changes as they occur. Some of the actors who disagreed with me, by the way, are fine actors, and I suspect that some of their fears may be groundless. Nonetheless, you must do what works for you. But you will learn what works for you only by trying things out.

For me, making associations at the beginning of my memorizing helped me learn the lines more efficiently and with more economy. There were no side effects later. That is all I need to know. If these devices free me of the burden of focusing on lines, and allow me to focus on objectives sooner, then more power to me. Once I am at ease with my lines, I am able to do a great range of things fearlessly and with abandon. I have always been able to use lines with ample flexibility—as my awareness of character and situation grows, and as those I work with change and grow. And of course, it is essential that an actor adjust to the requirements of the director as she discovers more about the play she is directing. The point is that you must learn for yourself what works for you and what doesn't. If you can use some of the memorization tools I have mentioned here without losing your ability to remain available to change, then I say go for it. If you cannot, then do what best works for you.

I also discovered in my memorization journey that learning the ideas behind the words and making connections between them expedited my learning process. So did examining my lines for the story they contain, for the subtext they imply, and for the cause-and-effect progression that they provide. If you look closely, the back-and-forth dialogue in any scene—and the contents of most monologues, for that matter—progresses in a cause-and-effect fashion, one line leading to another in a logical order. The logic may not be clear to the characters living in the moment, but to the actors playing them, it can and should be apparent. The playwright is writing a story based on conflict, and the conflict progresses through a scene, after all. I discovered that if I divide a scene's dialogue into sections—beginning, middle, and end, for instance—it helps me remember the story and its progression. This in turn helps me remember the lines, which, for the most part are linear and logically chronological.

That means that line by line, idea by idea, the combined words of the scene are like stepping stones that form a dramatic progression. These stepping stones of ideas are usually easy to remember, simply because one idea does lead to the next. This logical progression is like a built-in mnemonic device. It's like a connect-the-dots drawing—each idea leads to the next and next and next, and ultimately creates a clear picture, one that is easy to remember. And better yet, both for learning the lines and the acting of them, each of these dots tells its own little story, which also helps make each dot easier to remember and gives the actor specific things to picture and to act.

So the memorization of the lines and the acting of them ultimately need not be considered separate processes. You might also notice that the idea units you come up with are very consistent with the acting beats you discover as you analyze your dialogue while doing your actor's homework. Beats, you will recall, are the length of script during which you play a particular objective. The end of a beat is usually reached when as a character you win, you lose, you make a discovery, or you are interrupted by new information that causes you to change your objective. Recognizing beats is also a good way to separate your memorization into learnable chunks.

A short side note here. I often see actors running their lines for a scene in the lobby or hallway, either brushing up or trying to learn their dialogue before going to class or rehearsal. It sometimes strikes me as silly that these actors are running their lines by rote, rather than with acting commitment. Since the memorizing and the acting reinforce each other, why waste the opportunity to do both at once? There are several reasons for taking the rote-memorization approach, I suppose. Sometimes it's a matter of self-consciousness. Other times it's the fact that actors mistakenly believe that it takes more energy to act at the same time that they are running lines. But acting with intensity takes concentration, and good concentration usually means the lines come more easily. Still other times, actors are probably thinking that if they commit to a reading, they won't be able to undo that reading later—just like those actors I spoke of earlier. But it strikes me that if that logic holds, actors who say their lines flatly are learning to say their lines in that manner. Why are they not worried that *that* choice will be stuck in their memory? There is a logic disconnect here, no?

One final point about saying lines aloud as you learn them. I discovered as I was struggling to learn my own part that very often as I was digging for the next line; the process of searching for and finding that next line was not unlike what we do in life when we try to come up with the words that adequately express our feelings or thoughts. Ironically, as actors, once we get comfortable with our lines, they sometimes fall into a pattern that is almost musical; we know them so well that we no longer struggle in any way when we are called upon to say them. It is like we totally know what we need to say and how we are going to say it.

But for many of us in life, most of the time that is not the case. Unless we have specifically prepared what we are going to say, more often than not there remains an element of searching, of hesitation, of finding the right word or phrase or idea, and of discovering that we have done so. When we are able to retain this element in our acting, it often seems more improvised, spontaneous, and lifelike. I am not advocating for not knowing your lines well here. What I am saying is that this element of struggle you contend with when first learning the lines is worth remembering and using when it is appropriate to do so.

All right, now it's time for you to take a look at how some of these suggestions might actually work. What follows is a speech by Morty, one of the characters from the play *Shooting Blank's Verse,* a farce about a group of memory-challenged actors trying to get their play on its feet. Use the speech to explore some of the memorization suggestions cited above. Here is a list of things you might want to explore using the speech:

1. Read the speech several times looking for its story arc.
2. Then divide it into idea units.

3. Find its logical progression and isolate its dramatic stepping stones.
4. Picture specifically any images that the speech produces in you.
5. Use any feelings that the images and ideas produce in you.
6. You might even want to rewrite the speech in a form that separates its idea units visually. You might want to separate the piece into its opening, middle, and concluding sections, as well—to help you see the story arc in your mind.
7. Separate the speech into beats, if you can.
8. Try saying the speech aloud as you work.
9. Physicalize it if you wish.
10. Try any and all of the things that have been discussed in this text.

Now do some purposeful memorizing!

Morty: I suck! I suck! I can't effin' learn lines to save my life. People who can read words on the printed page, say them once, and parrot them back amaze me. And I know such people exist because my father is one of them. He reads a page of a script once or twice, and I swear he has it memorized. Completely memorized. What pisses me off even more is that he can actually still remember it a few hours later. Now that, my friend, is a gift. What a piece of magic. Imagine being an actor who doesn't have to go through that clumsy crap—tripping over words, panicking when you go blank. Imagine being able to focus on the other guy and actually listen to him without worrying about what you're gonna have to say next. Honest to God, that would be nirvana, that would be acting heaven.

Here is the speech again. This time I italicized images that I might work with to build memorable images and feelings. Doing so should help with memorization and with finding deeper specific moments.

> *I suck! I suck*! I can't *effin'* learn lines to save my life. People who can read words on the printed page, say them once, and *parrot them back* amaze me. And I know such people exist because *my father* is one of

> them. He reads a page of a script once or twice, and I swear he has it memorized. Completely memorized. *What pisses me off* even more is that he can actually still remember it a few hours later. Now that, my friend, is a gift. What a *piece of magic.* Imagine being an actor who doesn't have to go through that clumsy crap—*tripping over words, panicking when you go blank.* Imagine being able to focus on the other guy and actually listen to him without *worrying* about what you're gonna have to say next. Honest to God, that would be *nirvana*, that would be *acting heaven.*

Now here it is in possible idea units. Your ideas don't have to match mine. I've divided the speech into units that in my mind go easily together. Maybe you'll need a different fit.

> I suck! I suck!   I can't effin' learn lines to save my life.   People who can read words on the printed page, say them once,   and parrot them back amaze me. And I know such people exist   because my father is one of them.   He reads a page of a script once or twice,   and I swear he has it memorized.   Completely memorized.   What pisses me off even more is that he can actually still remember it a few hours later.   Now that, my friend, is a gift.   What a piece of magic.   Imagine being an actor who doesn't have to go through that clumsy crap   —tripping over words,   panicking when you go blank.   Imagine being able to focus on the other guy   and actually listen to him   without worrying about what you're gonna have to say next.   Honest to God,   that would be nirvana,   that would be acting heaven.

Finally, here's the speech in possible beats.

> I suck! I suck! I can't effin' learn lines to save my life. People who can read words on the printed page, say them once, and parrot them back amaze me.
>
> And I know such people exist because my father is one of them. He reads a page of a script once or twice, and I swear he has it memorized. Completely memorized. What pisses me off even more is that he can actually still remember it a few hours later.

> Now that, my friend, is a gift. What a piece of magic.
>
> Imagine being an actor who doesn't have to go through that clumsy crap—tripping over words, panicking when you go blank. Imagine being able to focus on the other guy and actually listen to him without worrying about what you're gonna have to say next.
>
> Honest to God, that would be nirvana, that would be acting heaven.

Your breaking down of the speech might have produced different results, but that's fine. The purpose here has been to see which devices work best for you, or work for you at all. Ask yourself the following:

> Which of the tools made your memorizing process easier, more economical? Why and how did they work for you?
>
> What refinements might you have been able to make that would have improved your memorization process even more?
>
> Did you discover that doing your actor's homework in this fashion helped you put the piece on its feet more quickly? With better acting results than if you used your regular grunt-it-out method of memorization? Why? How?

Whatever you learned about the way you memorize, begin to employ these techniques in your future memorization and acting homework. There are many, many other devices that I have not listed here, I'm sure. Some other very effective techniques you may discover on your own. Maybe you have already discovered some. If so, share them with your fellow actors. There is much that can be learned in this area. But most importantly, don't be afraid to try new things.

Regardless of what techniques ultimately work for you, never forget that what the playwright has written into the script is there for a reason. Each word, each phrase, and each mark of punctuation was put there by the playwright after careful deliberation and much painstaking love. You owe it to the playwright and to yourself as an artist to respect his choices and his craft. Learn your lines and deliver them the way they were written. It is very unlikely that your accidental changes will improve upon what is already there. I'm sure that Willy S. and Tennessee W. would wholeheartedly agree.

Here follows a list of memorization suggestions contributed by others or mentioned or implied in the chapter. Try them out as your time and energy allows.

1. Treat memory as you would a muscle. Do it regularly and get better at it. Increase the amounts you take on to memorize each day as your ability grows.
2. Find a time of day that best works for you to memorize. Consider that time sacred, and make sure you use your best time for memorizing whenever possible.
3. Memorize before you go to bed, and sleep on it.
4. Repeat lines in your head all through the day.
5. Read the lines over and over before trying to memorize them.
6. Learn the ideas and their interconnectedness before trying to memorize.
7. Learn the story of the lines before you learn the lines.
8. Say your lines aloud rather than in your head.
9. Say your lines aloud and in your head.
10. Say your lines while moving around.
11. Picture your lines as images as you say them.
12. Remember the feelings that the words and images create, not just the words.
13. Write your lines down before you memorize them. Write them as you are memorizing them.
14. See all of your lines in a scene as one big whole. Rewrite them as though they are a monologue. Examine this monologue in terms of its dramatic progression. Divide into its beginning section, middle section, and concluding section. Then divide each section into its constituent parts. Once you understand all of each section, and its cause-and-effect progression, then memorize.
15. Figure out what the character is actually saying when he says what he says, before trying to memorize it. (This is not the same thing as memorizing the way to say it. That should be avoided absolutely.)

16. Use mnemonic devices to help remember lists. Anagrams, rhymes, silly sentences, and song tunes, for instance, can be all effective.
17. Tape your part into a recorder, and once you have memorized sections, repeat it along with your taped version.
18. Learn the part by listening and reciting with your taped version.
19. Listen to your taped version and develop specific gestures, movements, and business that you actually do while listening. Eventually, the physicalities will help you remember the lines.
20. Memorize by beats. Learn a beat, add a beat, repeat the already learned beats, and add the new beat.

CHAPTER

TEN

RELAXATION AND EMOTION

THE PREVIOUS CHAPTER WAS ALL ABOUT MEMORIZATION — a subject I hadn't given much thought to as a teacher of acting. No longer true, obviously, as a result of my experiences dealing with major monologue obligations. Now here are two other subjects that I have given and, frankly, continue to give short shrift to as an acting teacher, but they are, despite my inattention, also critically important to your acting tool kit– craft elements that, like memorization, you must continue to develop on your own.

The subjects I am referring to are relaxation and emotion. Though there is no doubt in my mind that an actor must be relaxed to perform to her maximum efficiency, I have been willing to sacrifice its primacy in my own studio because there are so many other issues that seem more important. Emotion, or "the dreaded E word" as it is playfully referred to by my students, is something I have seldom given much direct time to in class on either the high school or undergraduate levels. Emotion, as I explain to my students, should come as a natural result of playing actions fully and completely, but it need not and should not be played directly. After my recent experience, however, I feel I must amend, just slightly, my feelings on feeling. We'll get to that later in this chapter.

RELAXATION

When I taught acting on the high school level, I usually started my acting classes with a warm-up, often a lengthy one. In my own training, I was taught that the relaxed body was one that could more easily live in the moment, be spontaneously responsive, and offer up the best possible work. As a performer I believed that wholeheartedly, and I have always made sure that I was properly prepared before I walked onto the stage.

I never liked the group warm-up, though. It usually made me self-conscious, or distracted me from truly committing to the relaxation exercises. We all have our quirks, and I have come to believe that we are responsible for finding and employing the relaxation and warm-up regimen best suited to our personal needs.

After I moved to college-level teaching, I eventually eliminated the warm-up from my classroom routine altogether (except for first-year students, as I will explain later). I came to feel that the limited time I had to spend with my actors was best devoted to scene work or other meat-and-potatoes content. It just became too difficult for me to give up a third of the class, which is how long it takes to conduct a meaningful warm-up. I rationalized that students needed to learn to be responsible for themselves and that if they needed a warm-up in order to produce their best work for class, it was their responsibility to take care of that before my class started. Spending less time would only produce a halfhearted warm-up, and one that was not necessarily suited to everyone. I still feel that way. But going through my recent rehearsal process and performance schedule as an actor reminded me of how important being relaxed and properly warmed up is.

Relaxation can be defined as the absence of the actor's greatest enemy—nerves. I relearned a lot about nerves during my return to acting. I was nervous all through the weeks I spent memorizing and preparing for the actual rehearsal process, so nervous, in fact, that whenever I tried to perform my speeches in front of my wife, I would lose the lines that I thought I knew backward and forward. Even when I was acting well, the lines would leave me because my nerves would weaken my concentration. The day I finally got through all of my part for her was an incredible relief. So you can imagine how nervous I was by the time I actually had to rehearse with a director and other actors. Only my preparation and my total concentration and commitment saved me from losing it altogether. No one knew, fortunately, but I struggled internally, believe me. In time, though, I began to enjoy rehearsals and to relax. That's when the good work really began to emerge.

I have seldom in my life been as scared, however, as I was on opening night of *White People.* I have always had a bit of stage fright—the kind that would quickly disappear after a few moments onstage—but the fear I felt prior to and during that first performance of *White People* was in a separate class.

I felt an incredible amount of pressure after fourteen years away from the stage. As an acting teacher, I had a reputation to protect, and I felt I had much to lose if I failed. I was filled with self-doubt and had deep and dark forebodings about forgetting my lines. (Actually, my fear about forgetting lines was not at all irrational, considering the enormous amount each of us had to remember, the briefness of the rehearsal period, the lack of time spent doing our work in front of an audience, and the fact that there was noplace to go to for help if any of us went up on a line, since this was a monologue play without interaction between characters.)

My fear on opening night was such that I found myself thinking about my lines at almost every moment through my first four of seven total speeches. My words sounded odd to me as I said them, making me feel that I had to closely monitor what I said. I felt like a fighter pilot trying to keep the target properly fixed in the crosshairs of my cockpit display. My performance would drift to the left or right of, and above or below, the target, as I made the slightest adjustments. I continuously felt that I might spin out of control at any time.

The problem was compounded by the fact that the opening-night audience responded to everything, and there was an incredible electric energy in the air. In the early going, the audience found me hilarious and they seemed to get everything I was saying even before I did. I had to adjust to their responses, which, of course, changed the timing of everything, making it that much more difficult to keep the target in front of me.

I found myself responding to the audience, as well I should, before thinking about doing so. Each of us in the cast spent about a third of the play, five to seven minutes at a time, speaking directly to the audience. So each change I would initiate affected and altered everything in each of my speeches that followed. Then in the later scenes, which are intensely charged with emotion, the audience's rapt attention seemed to magnify my every nuance to the point that I was conscious of the emotion that was spontaneously coming from me. It crossed my mind that I was pushing to get a reaction, and I began to doubt that what was happening to me would seem real and believable to the audience. Yet they remained totally engaged. I could feel them.

At the end of the play my character's emotional outpouring reaches a crescendo as he tells the story of his son's involvement in a racial hate crime. When it was over, there was a frighteningly long silence followed by a thunderous ovation. In spite of the anxieties I'd had all night, the play was very well received and so was the work of all the actors, including mine. In spite of my nerves, in spite of never feeling totally merged into the moments of the play, I came off as relaxed, natural, and spontaneous. (I know this from the audience's response, from the published reviews, and because people who saw the show and know better than to jive me have told me it is true.) I can credit this only to my ability to ignore the internal distractions and concentrate on what I needed to do. Though my internal experience was certainly not the ideal one, the audience never suspected that I was a struggling fighter pilot perilously close to losing control and crashing.

I believe that meeting the challenge of performance in spite of my nerves was the result of training, self-discipline, and proper preparation for entering the playing area. These are values and skills that are worth addressing in the classroom, even though in the last several years I have spent little time doing so. In my program, students get relaxation and warm-up work in their voice and speech classes and their movement classes. (First-year students get it in my acting class, as well.) But I believe that once introduced to these techniques, it becomes your responsibility to develop them so that they serve you effectively. This takes practice and commitment.

It is up to you to discover what works best for you, what you need to do in terms of time to make these tools work for you, and then commit the necessary time to get relaxed and focused. Further, I think it is your responsibility to take the time, even if it is time you must find outside of class, to get yourself ready to work at your best level. Ultimately, you must find your own way. Each of us is different, and each of us must find and put into practice what we need to do in terms of preparation to produce the necessary work. Your training may not offer you all the things required to get you to your own state of maximum acting efficiency. I believe it is your obligation to accept the importance of doing so and then rely on self-discipline to get to that point. This may also mean further independent exploration outside the classroom or studio to find additional techniques. If you intend to become a serious master of your craft, this should be obvious to you.

In my freshman acting class, I teach warm-up exercises as a how-to part of the acting class at the beginning of their first semester. As I mentioned, the voice and movement teachers do that, as well. I remind students that what they are looking for during their training is a way to build a vocabulary of exercises that will work for them individually as they move toward the profession. I let them know that it is their responsibility to commit to any exercises they are introduced to so they can discover the ones that really are most effective for them. I also make sure to offer up a variety of relaxation exercises, including meditative ones, so that my students are introduced to the range of possibilities. I emphasize that no one thing works for everyone. Here follows a list of books from a variety of relaxation sources that have been helpful to me. It is by no means a complete list, but if your own training has not included exposure to relaxation methodology, this list can help you begin your own education.

Body Wisdom: The Use and Training of the Human Body Arthur Lessac

Freeing the Natural Voice Kristin Linklater

The Actor Speaks Patsy Rodenburg

Laban for Actors and Dancers Jean Newlove

The Actor at Work Robert L. Benedetti

Acting through Exercises John L. Gronbeck-Tedesco

Voice and the Actor Cicely Berry

Awareness through Movement Moshe Feldenkrais

The Language of the Body Alexander Lowen

Self-Mastery through Self-Hypnosis Roger H. Bernhardt and David Lozell Martin

Creative Visualization Shakti Gawain

Free Play Stephen Nachmanovitch

Creating a Character: A Physical Approach to Acting Moni Yakim

The Way of Acting Tadashi Suzuki

The Moving Body Jacques Lecoq

The Expressive Body David Alberts

I sometimes notice even with my college students that there is a lack of discipline and preparation prior to beginning daily rehearsals and in performance. Students will show up for rehearsals just at the call time and then not be ready to work when the rehearsal actually begins. In productions I have directed, particularly in plays with larger casts, I have seen noisy carryings-on in dressing rooms that would certainly be distracting to me if I were about to perform. Granted, there are those who need absolutely no preparation before hitting the stage, but I believe the majority of performers need to prepare for their first entrance and stay focused throughout, particularly when doing a serious piece of work.

It is your obligation to yourself, to your fellow actors, and to the audience to make your every entrance properly prepared to do so. For that reason I always address my cast before dress rehearsals begin. I remind them first of what is expected of them in terms of conduct and then in respect for fellow actors' work. If they do not maintain a level of respect for each other in the dressing room, they hear about it. If their work suffers onstage because of a lack of preparation, they hear about it. I also talk in class about preparing before performing scene work and encourage my students to get to class early enough so they'll be ready when the work begins.

Each of the three Equity actors who made up the company of *White People* warmed up before every performance. The youngest of us, a guy in his midtwenties and three years out of Carnegie Mellon, had his own routine based primarily on Linklater. He had to yell a lot in the play, so he was most concerned with his vocal relaxation and spent most of his time working on his voice. The second actor in my company was a woman in her early forties who was a certified Linklater teacher. She took herself through a complete menu of physical and vocal exercises each night and always recited the lines to her first monologue. I always did my entire script aloud before coming to the theatre and repeated my lines again on my way to the theatre in the car. Forgetting my lines continued to be a primary concern for me, so it was relaxing for me each day to know that I could still say them all. I also meditated for twenty minutes at some point before each show. At the theatre, I always got onstage before half-hour to gently flex my voice and to move through my blocking. We performed in a small theatre and our physical action was limited, so my big concern was just feeling relaxed—and, of course, the words. The point here is that each of us recognized the importance of relaxation before going onstage. Each of us had our own way of preparing, and each of us adjusted our regimen to the specific requirements of the show we were performing.

Keep in mind that physical, vocal, and emotional preparedness are all intertwined. If physically or vocally we are tight, it will affect our emotional availability. If emotionally we are not relaxed, it will affect our bodies.

Therefore it is essential that we get the whole mechanism down to neutral. I have always done a physical and vocal warm-up before performing onstage. When I am nervous, my voice tends to sit in a much higher range than when I am relaxed. It adds to my discomfort when I notice the thinness of the sound I'm producing. I feel it is less commanding, I feel less in control, and I am aware that my vocal range is compromised. Becoming aware of my tension makes me even more nervous.

When I am not relaxed, my body feels heavy and unresponsive. I become clumsy and self-conscious. Even the simplest physical task becomes complex and uncomfortable. I remember that in rehearsals, pouring a glass of scotch required an abnormal amount of concentration. I had to speak at the same time, and it seemed as difficult as juggling four balls and a chain saw while eating an apple. Under these circumstances, how could I possibly create the illusion that my character was relaxed? How could I possibly put my energy into communicating with the audience?

As rehearsals progressed, however, I became more and more comfortable with the physical action required of me, and I noted that though my voice might feel reedy when I started out, my concentration was so strong that my voice relaxed and lowered before much time had elapsed. By the time I was well rehearsed, the physical and vocal requirements of the role in the small theatre we were to play in had become insignificant. It was my emotional relaxation alone that remained a concern. No matter how much I warmed up physically, no matter how I got my body and voice to seem relaxed, on the inside I was still scared to death, and it was a distraction. Meditation helped, but it did not provide me with a cure.

In desperation, shortly before we opened I finally asked a therapist friend who uses hypnosis if he had any ideas. He was able to provide me with some imaging techniques that gave me some relief. But one particular exercise involving a combination of deep breathing, sighing, and a set of eyeball rolls actually brought me palpable and instant relief. I found if I did this exercise about fifteen minutes before curtain time it was like taking a tranquilizer. It worked so well that if I did it any closer to curtain time it would have compromised my energy level in a negative way. The discovery of this exercise was a godsend. It allowed me to function as a normal human being during the first week of our run, when, I'm embarrassed to admit, I otherwise would have remained a complete basket case. As the show moved through its run, of course, the realization that I was surviving and actually flourishing allowed me to relax more and more, and by the end of the run I felt pretty close to normal even before working my warm-up.

The point of all this is that every actor must hit the stage in as close to a relaxed state as possible in order to be able to produce her best work. Ultimately, it is your individual responsibility to find a way to discover and maintain that state. Your teachers cannot accomplish this goal for you. Our individual physical, emotional, and vocal makeup simply varies so much that this is an obligation that you will have to take on and work through independently and over time.

And now a little coda to this section on relaxation.

In spite of my preparations to avoid it, I went up in a performance during the first week of production. Completely. Though I knew where I was in the story and even why I lost the line, in my panic I simply could not find my way back to the words. I stood there frozen for a moment, but still no dialogue came to me. In desperation, I started to engage in some extemporaneous stage action that seemed appropriate for my character while I ran through the lines of my script in my head. When I finally found the lost string, I began again. My colleagues told me that what I had done covered my going up seamlessly and assured me that most of the audience did not even realize what had happened. Internally, however, I died a thousand deaths.

By the fourth week of the run, when it happened again, I was able to ad-lib the story until the lines came back to me. There was no panic, no anguish this time, because I was truly relaxed onstage. My biggest worry (besides looking like a fool) throughout the entire rehearsal period and opening of the show was forgetting the lines. Yet when I was relaxed enough, even the coming to pass of that nightmare became no more than a temporary blip on the radar screen. What I learned then was that the powerful effect of being relaxed when performing cannot be emphasized enough.

EMOTION

I tell my students constantly that they must not focus on emotion. I try to get them to think of emotion as a byproduct of their work. Concentrate on actions and objective, I tell them over and over again. Probably because I'm so emphatic on this point, sometimes my students misunderstand and think I'm telling them that emotion is not part of what an actor should do. This, of course, is not at all what I am saying. What I *am* saying is that a focus on emotion, at the expense of telling the story clearly and effectively, will not serve the production or the character. But many of my students were shocked when they came to see me in *White People.* There I was displaying extreme emotion all over the place. The role required it if I was going to tell the best possible story. The emotion had to be real. It had to be raw. And it had to be reliably there.

One of the things I came to realize while I was rehearsing and playing in this show is that relaxation and emotion are very closely connected for the actor, and that the ability to attain the former will strongly affect the ability to produce the latter. For me, being able to connect emotionally while onstage depended primarily not on emotional recall, not on substitution, but on relaxation. Here's what I'm talking about.

Before formal rehearsals began, I would spend a couple of hours every day going through my lines and, when ready, acting my entire part without stopping. With no one watching, I was brilliant. I could find new moments of inspiration every time I went through the piece. Physically I was loose, continuously finding new movement, gestures, and even occasional business that added to my characterization and to the ongoing story. Fortunately, after each run-through, I was smart enough to catalog what worked and what didn't and took a few moments to rehearse the things I had found so they would still be there the next time I worked the piece through. If I discovered things that physically or intellectually triggered emotions in me, and if the emotions were appropriate for where I was going with the piece at that particular moment, I would note the cause-and-effect sequence and rehearse those moments, too.

If I understood why a particular action or way of saying something triggered a particular emotional response, that would help me remember it as I moved through the script the next time. This cause-and-effect understanding would aid me in setting up the moment so I wouldn't have to force it or even think about it when it came again. But I was so relaxed during these run-throughs that new things were always spontaneously replacing old things, or, depending on how I was feeling on a particular day, a moment might go one way or another. A change in one moment would sometimes affect how the next several might be played out—never, though, at the sacrifice of the overall story I needed to be telling.

Let me give you an example. There was a moment late in *White People* when my character was talking about his son, who has committed a hate crime against a young African American couple. He had apparently written a hate-filled note in which he spelled the most common American racial slur incorrectly—with only one G. I said the line, "He couldn't even spell that right." Sometimes I found myself saying the line with tremendous anger directed at my son, not for having bad spelling, but for everything he's done. I used the line to attack him. Other times when I said the line, the emotion of self-pity and failure came over me and it produced a completely different moment and showed a completely different side of my character. Each worked well, because each of these directions was emotionally connected and moving. Neither compromised the ongoing story. Since I was well rehearsed, knew what I had to do overall, and was totally relaxed, my spontaneous response took over and produced a lovely moment. What a pleasure it was to find myself working like this.

When I tried to do the same kind of work for my first preview audience, my patient wife, I was so nervous that it was all but impossible to let myself commit to the moments as they happened. My own concerns about how she would react completely overwhelmed my ability to let things happen. I could barely remember the lines, for God's sake. Fortunately, though, by the time I first revealed my work to her, I was already so well rehearsed, so knowledgeable about what I was doing, that even though I couldn't relax and be in the moment, even though I was struggling with my lines, there was still enough core good work there that she was buying, even as I was dying.

By the third time I attempted to perform the piece for her from beginning to end, I was relaxed enough, at least for stretches at a time, to truly be in some moments. When I got to the big emotional stuff I was so relieved that I began to cry spontaneously with an intensity that I never achieved onstage. It was me crying, not the character, because I was so relieved to have finally been so connected while someone else was watching.

Though I never achieved that degree of spontaneous emotion onstage, I always was able to generate honest emotion without pushing for it, performance after performance, and I believe that I was always able to move the audience in the way the playwright wanted them to be moved. Ultimately, it is the actor's primary job to make the audience feel, not to make himself feel. I honestly believe I never failed to do my job, even when, as on opening night, my inner voice was distractingly all over the place. How well I did it on any given night depended largely on how relaxed I was. When I was relaxed enough to be able to do my job as I rehearsed it, when I was able to concentrate adequately on what I needed to do rather than be pulled by what I was feeling emotionally myself, I could act well. But no matter how much I rehearsed, if I could not relax enough to focus on the essentials of my job, my work would always be less than it might have been. That is why relaxation is essential.

As the run progressed, the same kind of spontaneous in-the-moment creativity that I described about my solo rehearsals began to take place in front of and because of the audience. Since the three actors in *White People* had to address the audience directly throughout the play, we were really engaged in a dialogue with them. Each audience we played to was different, of course, and each responded to our work differently. Playing off the various audiences and their reactions each night helped each of us further define our characters and find new ways of playing moments. As my ability to relax increased, so did my ability to take risks by engaging, challenging, and provoking the audience.

At the beginning of the run, I avoided looking directly at any particular audience member. I was afraid that what I saw might unnerve me. But as the run progressed, I began using individuals; I tried to provoke them, make them laugh, make them feel uncomfortable, or make them accept or reject me overtly. When they did so, they would react spontaneously, and it was real. I could use that to make my next moment, and I would, sometimes producing new moments that I didn't know were there, great moments, in fact. Sometimes these were moments that could never be repeated; other times what I learned could be applied in a new way with another audience. But all this was possible, again, only because I was relaxed enough to listen with all my senses, just as actors do when they are reacting to each other in a play that allows for character interaction onstage behind the fourth wall.

Finally I realized I had relearned for myself what I am always telling actors in my class. You rehearse and rehearse until you don't have to think about it anymore. You know the lines, you know the blocking, you know the actions you will have to play. You know what you need, and you know the strategies for getting what you need. You have rehearsed it for so long, you know it so well, that it is in your bones. That's when you forget about it and live in the moment. And that, of course, is when the best acting occurs. This, as an actor, is what you shoot for. This is why you do all the preliminary work and commit fully to getting your lines and actions down. This is the art of the craft that should be your goal. But what my return to the stage reminded me was that you can accomplish that goal only when you are relaxed enough to do so. And when you can, the emotional truth, and the creativity that makes acting an art as well as a craft, comes most powerfully into play.

There is a subtle point here, one that I would actually be hesitant to make to my own acting students. From the start of my rehearsal process, I began to make decisions about where, emotionally, my character might be at any given time in the story. I was never married to an emotional response, but my analysis of the story certainly suggested to me where many big moments were in terms of both action and emotion. These choices came as a result of taking a look at the play from the audience's point of view and considering what I might want to see at particular points in the story arc. There will be a lot more on this in the next chapter.

What my reading told me was that I had to be ready to make the big emotional response at those points, so I found things during rehearsal that would help me get there. In rehearsals, I might make the choice to yell, to drink, to wave my hand, to point my finger accusingly. Sometimes, in my personal rehearsals especially, I forced myself to go for an emotional effect, and I practiced until I could feel comfortable doing so without any pushing. Then the moment settled in and, in time, evolved with the genuine feelings that I was producing.

The truth is I was doing what I tell my students not to do: I was shaping the story arc in rehearsal by pursuing an emotional effect. The difference is that I am a fairly skilled and experienced actor, and I realized that it was part of a process and not going to be the ultimate product. Sometimes actors confuse process with product. That is when the result turns out to be a pushed and artificial package of unbelievable emotional simulations. That is why leading with emotion is seldom a good approach to take. However, keeping in mind that you must examine your work from the vantage point of what the audience will see is always a good idea.

A final word on emotional recall and substitution. Like most of my students, you're probably very interested in and confused by these topics. I discuss how these techniques are used when the topics come up in class, but we never focus on it as a subject. So the question is, did I ever use these techniques while rehearsing or performing my emotional role? The answer is yes. In rehearsals, I always tried to find parallels between my two children in

White People, a son and a daughter, and my own fourteen-year-old daughter. When I could find parallels between situations, it helped me understand what my character might be thinking and feeling and doing at a particular time. I used those feelings, when I could find them specifically, for a starting point in my acting choices. Also, because I had several minutes between speeches in performance, though I always remained onstage, I was able to use things from my own life that emotionally would get me where I wanted to be before I spoke again. I also used what my fellow actors were saying and doing onstage, often emotionally charged things, when they fed into what I was going for. The trick here was that I had time to employ these triggering devices. I never tried to use them as in-the-moment tools. I agree with Stella Adler's take on these internal acting approaches. How can you be in the moment if you're busy substituting or thinking about yourself?

In the end, though, my experience doing *White People* was probably not totally reflective of what it might have been like doing a more ordinary play. A monologue situation is specialized and requires that acting skills take on a different order of importance than in a play where characters are dealing with each other. Nonetheless, it is part of the actor's craft to be able to reach into his tool kit of technique and use those things that will best serve him at any particular time. I discovered, happily, that my years of teaching have sharpened and increased my ability to do that effectively.

CHAPTER
ELEVEN

PUTTING YOUR SOLO TOGETHER

THE SECOND HALF OF THIS BOOK HAS FOCUSED ON LONG-range goals of craft—things that you must continue to work on as you develop your skills. That is not to say that you don't continue to work on the craft items discussed in the first half. But in the first section of the book, we were mostly talking about specific application of craft to specific kinds of material. In the second half of *Acting Solo,* we have discussed craft in terms of the broader issues that actors face every time they set out to do a role in a production. These issues include analysis, of course, but also things like memorization, relaxation, and the use of emotion in acting. Now let's take a look at how all the elements of craft discussed in this book intersect when an actor is actually working on a part.

As you probably gathered from the last few chapters, my return to acting after a fourteen-year hiatus started out less than joyfully. I had allowed a few insignificant items—like feeling deathly afraid of failure—to compromise my excitement. I was petrified at the possibility of failing, or embarrassing myself, and especially of looking bad in front of my peers, colleagues, and students. I had worked hard on my teaching and directing in the years since my last stage venture, and a part of me feared I could destroy a reputation established through years of committed work.

Though I had lost my confidence as an actor, I was soon to discover that I had built a body of acting craft far superior to what I possessed before I began those fourteen years of teaching. More importantly, the craft I had learned would carry me through even though my lack of confidence would try to betray me. This is the most important theme I have been trying to convey throughout this book. The craft you master will always serve you. It will be your life jacket, your parachute, your map. In possession of a solid system of craft, the things you can actually master despite your limitations, you really cannot fail. Here, then, is a review of the things you can master as seen through my own experience using my own life jacket.

SCRIPT ANALYSIS

The acting process must always begin with the script.

No doubt, my ability to analyze a script served me extremely well in my return to the stage. If you have been paying attention throughout this book, you realize by now that my emphasis is always on the actor's responsibility for telling the story the playwright has provided—believably and compellingly. I have always stressed that to accomplish this goal, it is essential that the actor first be able to analyze the script efficiently, and then be able to make and execute a series of choices that will effectively tell the story based on that analysis. Instinct and intuition come later. Of course, as an actor you must be believable, as well, but you can complete your mission only by making choices that are clear, compelling, and in line with the script. When you do this, you ensure that your work will be exciting, but never at the expense of the overall intentions of the playwright. This is how I approached my own responsibility in the production I was about to become a part of.

As you recall, *White People* by J. T. Rogers is a full-length play without intermission. It is populated by three characters who never interact with each other onstage. Each of the characters speaks for about thirty to thirty-five minutes, addressing the audience but never each other. Though each of their long monologues is actually in continuous time, their speeches have been broken up by the playwright and divided into six or seven sections, depending on the part. Each of the characters speaks in approximately five- to seven-minute chunks, at which point another character picks up where he or she previously left off. Each of the character's monologues is linked to the others only by the general themes of the play and by the fact that the focus for each character derives from a problem related to a son or daughter.

In the case of my character, Martin Bahmueller, a son has committed a violent hate crime against a young black couple. As a result, Martin, a high-powered corporate lawyer, is forced to leave his job and confront, though indirectly, his own veiled prejudices and his indirect complicity in his son's actions. Each of the other characters confronts the terrible residue of his or her own beliefs, as well, and as more and more of the onion skin surrounding their situations is peeled away, each tries desperately to come to terms with the insidious pain and grief caused by his or her poisonous beliefs.

Note that the preceding paragraph was a difficult one for me to write. Without going into a lot of detail, I wanted you to get what the play is about, how it works, and who my character was and give you enough to understand the comments on analysis I will soon be making. The paragraph was hard work because I had to select a set of core items to share with you, from the multitude of information I could have offered up. If I told you everything, you would have been overloaded and not have known what is important. If I told you too little or the wrong things, you would not understand what will soon follow. The point here is that if I have been successful, the victory comes as a result of understanding what the play is about and how it works—through its themes, its action or story, and its characters and dialogue. This process of isolating *White People*'s mechanics and choosing to communicate only its most important essentials is not easy. But it was necessary that I do so, if my communication to you was to be clear, compelling, and economical.

This is exactly the kind of process you must go through when you prepare a role. Though it is not an easy process to master, the skills required are learnable. And you must learn them essentially own your own. Most acting classes focus on what you are doing in the now, not on how you came to be doing it. Somehow, acting classes, for the most part, don't focus on the analysis part of the craft, yet there is always the assumption that you as an actor are able to make choices based on your reading of the script. For most of us, this is not any more automatic than reading. Most of us need to spend the time learning how to do it. I will return to this point later.

Analysis was certainly the approach I used– as I began to tackle my seven long and daunting monologues. The good news for me was that the necessary analysis came fairly easily to me, much more easily than it might have fourteen years ago. I believe this to be the result of my years of teaching analysis as part of the acting craft. Mastery of the elements of craft come more easily when you are responsible for teaching it to others. You really have to understand it to teach it effectively.

There is no doubt that knowing what to look for, knowing how to find it, and knowing how to use what I found made my early work on the script both economical and effective. In the previous two chapters I noted how memorization, relaxation, and emotion affected my ability to first come to terms with and then execute a series of choices that would ultimately lead me to my performance. Each of these items, not normally topics in my teaching toolbox, proved to be essential in the crafting and refining of my work. As I explained in those earlier chapters, my actual rehearsal would consist of only one week, including all run-throughs and dress rehearsals.

It was therefore incumbent on me to arrive at my first official rehearsal memorized and having already made the bulk of my acting choices. There would be no time for casual discovery and refinement with a director. My analysis choices, by necessity, quickly merged with my memorization process, and my memorization process merged with my process for making physical choices. Physical action helped me memorize and at the same time helped me find and more clearly define acting moments that my analysis might have already suggested. When I was relaxed, everything came to me more readily, and my imagination and my in-the-moment sensibilities helped make creative and useful things happen. In turn, my personal rehearsal process further helped me discover what I had, to that point, missed in the script. I was then able to translate any new discoveries into the final choices I would be bringing to my first official rehearsal. All that on my own. All that acting solo.

Here is a sampling of what the critics had to say, ultimately, about the play and my work in it:

> J. T. Rogers' *White People,* a trio of interlaced monologues with the common theme of racism, is theater that makes you squirm. It denies escapism and demands engagement, makes you think and feel and recoil. The play is, by turns, funny, sad, disturbing and terrific. In another strong production from Coral Gables' New Theatre and director Rafael de Acha, three fiercely powerful actors are illuminating the lives of people who have little more in common than the hue of their skin and a racism that they struggle to express, suppress, shape or justify. —*The Miami Herald*

> *White People* is significant for two reasons. First, Rogers serves up the subject of racial prejudice with downright ugly impact. This is no feel-good "why can't we be friends" message. Rogers's white people range from fearfully angry at worst to stunned and bewildered at best. There are no answers here, but the questions revealed are stark indeed. The second blessing is the chance to catch three fine performances in what really could be termed a spoken opera. The cast is strong, but Miller is outstanding. He plays the attorney in a fast-talking monotone, managing the difficult feat of making a humorless character seem very funny, but when the scarier aspects of the lawyer's tale are finally revealed, Miller really grabs you by the throat. —*New Times*

> *White People* addresses racial and ethnic differences in a way that demands confrontation, but without creating easy scapegoats. The New Theatre's powerful showcase is an engrossing experience that deliberately sneaks up on you, and leaves you arguing with yourself long after it's over. —*Sun Sentinel*

> And there is Martin Bahmueller (Bruce Miller), an attorney who recently moved from the Northeast to St. Louis, in part for the safety of his family, which he seems to find in the racially homogeneous suburbs. If Miller stands out among them (the cast), it is because his button-down, smug, most overtly racist character could easily drift into caricature. He keeps the guy grounded in reality, even as the rug gets pulled out from under him. —*Palm Beach Post*

Please note that I struggled a bit over whether to use these quotes or not. The point to using them was not to blow my horn, but to make a point. During my years as a professional actor, experience taught me not to read what critics had to say, but this time around, since I was told that all the criticism was positive, I decided to indulge. If you look beneath the kindness, though, what the critics are really referring to with their words about me is the craft that I applied in the preparation and performance of my work, mostly a result of script analysis and synthesis. I have never considered myself a particularly good actor, but despite my nerves, despite my lack of confidence, I had never felt so literally able to craft a performance—all based on what I had learned about using a script specifically and efficiently during my years of teaching.

With that in mind, let's take a closer look at the process I took myself through before actual rehearsals began. It is a system that works; it is a system that is reliable. That is what you should be looking for.

THE STEPS OF ANALYSIS

What exactly, was the story I was going to be telling? That was the question with which I began my analysis. For many actors, especially student actors, finding the essential story is no easy task, but in the particular case of *White People,* it might prove even harder, since the playwright's device was to mask the important story threads for as long as possible for each of the characters. In the seven speeches I had to deliver, the first three, I quickly discovered, offered no direct information about the specific problems in my character's life or what the driving conflict for him actually was. Only at the end of the fourth speech does he directly admit that there is a problem between his son and himself. Only in the fifth does he begin to reveal that his own place in the world is one that causes him trouble and gives him incredible pain. And it is not until the sixth and seventh speeches that the awful truth of his situation becomes graphically clear. Yet it is these late-inning revelations that fuel the character through the entire play. It is these late-inning revelations that have given him the overwhelming need to speak, in this case, to the audience, from the beginning of his first appearance onstage.

Once the mechanics of the script had become clear to me through my analysis, the breadcrumbs that had been dropped by the playwright and his character in the earlier speeches made themselves apparent. And once I understood the overall idea of how the plot worked, I was ready to go back and chart it specifically. I would need to find the cause-and-effect, step-by-step progression of the character through the story, no easy matter since the playwright had intentionally hidden so much beneath the onion skin of my character's self-denial, righteousness, and ego. But I knew if I could find and map out my journey through the story, I would have a clear arc or throughline to enact for an audience.

Mapping the throughline or story arc would, to a large degree, evolve from being able to identify and isolate any big moments that my character has. These moments would be the stepping stones for a clearly rendered dramatic progression that an audience could see—even if they were not realizing it at the time. I would need to find moments of victory and defeat, moments of discovery, and any other moments that might cause my character a change in direction, emotion, or intent. These moments, when linked together, would provide me with a connect-the-dots picture of my story arc—in each of the speeches individually, and throughout my character's journey, speech by speech.

With a close study of my script, I was eventually able to determine what and where many of these moments were. It would next become my job to find a way to emphasize these points, where necessary, for the audience. The audience would need to be able to recall these nuggets later in the play when their importance would be made clear, but the audience should not be dwelling on them before that time. This would be a delicate balance. The trick, I determined, would be to lay them out clearly without drawing undue attention.

By the fifth of seven speeches, the growing but still scattered patches of jigsaw parts that make up the script start congealing and begin to suggest a picture that is both dramatic and ugly. The more my character talks, the more closely the patches of picture move toward each other and toward a clarity necessitated by the climax to come. The accumulated suggestions provided in the script should trigger the imagination, so that the audience will be able to fill in much of the rest—when the time comes.

In the end, as one of the critics cited above mentioned, I chose to deliver much of my earlier stuff in a rapid-fire, confident manner that bordered on funny. Though I felt the importance of all of what I said as a character, as an actor I realized that playwright Rogers had provided in the actual lines of his script most of what was necessary, particularly in the early going. I needed no extra mustard in the delivery. Coming to understand when to sell and when to lay back is a matter of understanding the mechanics of drama—something that a skilled actor must develop and, ultimately, possess. This, too, must become part of your overall analysis process.

Once again, it is my belief that being able to tell the story effectively should be one of the primary goals, if not *the* primary goal, in your craft. Yet, as I mentioned earlier, many acting teachers feel analysis is a part of the analysis class, and only the moment-to-moment interaction linked to the playing of selected actions should be the focus in scene study. I disagree. I believe that when a student is left to master analysis outside the acting class, it seldom is mastered.

If you are going to be successful, you must understand how the playwright has laid out his story and then find ways of providing the physical enactment of this story through what you do, physically and verbally. This is called *analysis* and *synthesis.* Being able to do all this independently allowed me to begin my first rehearsal well prepared to work, because I already understood what I needed to do. You must be able to do this work on your own, because there is never a guarantee that a director will provide you with what you need. Nor is there ever a guarantee that a rehearsal schedule will provide the time and opportunity for you to stumble upon all the ingredients necessary for producing the level of work you want and will be expected to produce. That was certainly true in my case. And that is why so much of my own work was done before I stepped into the rehearsal studio for the first time.

All right; the story was now clear to me, and I could isolate what I considered to be its most important moments. It then became my responsibility to define each of those moments more specifically through how I would say and color the lines, through how I would fill them emotionally, and by the physical actions I would select and execute. A good deal of this aspect of my preparation was covered in the previous chapters. In summary, though, the more I learned about the script, the more reshaping, editing, and revamping I found myself doing.

I should probably point out that all of my preparation time was challenging, fun, and exciting. Even the memorizing, once I got past the fear factor, became an adventure. If you don't feel the same way about your work, you are probably spending your time in the wrong place. I believe it is important that you think about this. If what motivates you is some obligation you feel to pursue acting, even when if it does not make you feel good to do so, you are probably making a terrible mistake. Theatre is just plain too hard if love and joy are not your motivating factors.

Now back to the process. What was it, specifically, that I did to define and refine the lines I would be saying and the story I would be telling in performance? First, of course, there was the analysis. There was also the music of the lines as written by the playwright. J. T. Rogers's use of tempos, rhythms, and vocabulary specific to each character was very helpful, and since I recognized it, I was able to use these elements to build and shape my work. Then there was the breaking down of the lines themselves, looking for operatives, clues to character, and a shaping of the speeches to ensure they had beginnings, middles, and ends with appropriate dramatic builds. As one critic noted, there was an operatic quality to the writing provided by Rogers. The actors couldn't ignore these aspects of the provided script.

After all this, of course, there remained the task of relating the script to the objective-playing and physical-action choices I would need to make—a subject that I will go into more deeply in a few moments. In another kind of play, where I would be sharing the stage with other actors and would not be dealing with solo monologues, the issues of objective playing would probably have been dealt with earlier in my process because of the interaction between characters. But since in *White People* I would be working alone, mastering the words on the page and how they would be used on the audience was the primary task. Since I had no audience to rehearse with, the normal order of preparation was, by necessity, altered.

The overriding point here, if not already obvious, is that script analysis was the source of all of my work and of my ability to work efficiently on my own. Though I was operating under special circumstances for this production, my return to the stage reinforced my belief that the ability to use a script efficiently is the cornerstone of a reliable actor's craft.

ACTIONS AND OBJECTIVES

Now let's take a closer look at my use of one of the most basic tools of the craft and certainly a major ingredient in my own teaching—the playing of actions or objectives. *Objectives* refer to what a character needs at every moment of her stage time and what she should be trying to attain at every moment. Since this need is derived from the conflict the playwright has provided, it follows that this need or objective can be obtained only from another character sharing the stage at any particular time. That character will be holding up his end of the playwright's provided conflict by trying to fulfill his own need. In the usual play, the formula is *find the conflict and determine the objective.*

The problem in *White People,* however, is the fact that each character is alone onstage. There are no other characters to provide obstacles and conflict. There is only the audience and what is going on inside each of the characters individually—intellectually and emotionally. But since the play is written with the convention that the characters are actually talking to the audience as the audience, the question became: why is each character doing so, and what does each character need from that audience?

In some plays, and often in monologue work, where the actor finds herself addressing the audience, that audience is being used as a stand-in for a listening friend, the psychiatrist, or her mother, and so forth. This is an awkward device that requires the actor to imagine someone who isn't really there and send it out through the audience, . This is not the case in *White People*. Each of the actors is actually using the audience as the audience—one of those suspension-of-disbelief conventions that only theatre can get away with. But during my preparation, obviously, I had no audience to work with, so I had to imagine what their reactions might be, and make my reactions to their reactions based on my inferences. And there was no guarantee that what I imagined was what I would get in performance. I would need to be ready to make in-the moment adjustments when an audience finally did make an appearance.

What I could do in the meantime was try to determine what it was I wanted from the audience during my journey through the play and how I could attain that goal through the delivery of my lines. Since the play centers on the prejudice that is a central part of the makeup of each of the characters, it would be a logical jump to think these characters might be looking for approval, or trying to prove the virtue of their beliefs, or at least getting the audience to understand where they are coming from. But each of the characters in the play treats the audience as though the audience already agrees with his or her belief system. As a result, none of these choices would work. Ultimately, I determined that what my character wanted, overall, was to get the audience to help him understand why his son might have done what he did, and to get reassurance that he was not responsible for his son's actions. Since my character spends so little time actually talking about his son, getting the audience to see how great Martin is was a tactic I used much of the time in shaping my role. Asserting and justifying my ego was something that I could build on. It was also justified in the script.

There was danger in this approach, however. I would be building a character who is not likable. Would the ending of the play be emotionally powerful if the audience didn't like Martin? How much did the audience need to like him to make the play work? How would the choices I made affect how the audience thought of Martin, and how could I monitor the effectiveness of my choices without the benefit of an actual audience? Regretfully, I realized that while working on my own, I would not be able to determine an audience's reaction, but I knew that my character, even as written, was not likable. I also realized that I would have to find a way to give the audience enough to care about me whether they liked me or not. Since I was using ego as a central character choice, I decided I would have to temper Martin's off-putting qualities with other, more positive qualities. I settled on giving him a sense of humor, and a love for his family that could be demonstrated throughout the performance. I found many places in the script where I could do these things, so demonstrating these qualities to the audience became part of my objective. I knew, of course, that all my choices awaited the eyes of a director, whose function, among others, would be to represent the eyes and ears of an audience. I would need him to tell me whether I had found enough balance in my character for there to be a dramatically appropriate payoff at the climax of the play.

Making these kinds of character choices, psychological and physical, is where you must add to what is given you on the page and where your own creativity comes into play. All of these creative choices, however, must still be based on and consistent with what has been provided by the script and must be used to serve it.

And now some notes on my process for finding physical choices.

PHYSICALLY SERVING THE STORY AND THE CHARACTER

I knew from the outset that I would have very little room to work with in performance. The New Theatre is a tiny space. I also knew that the director had two options. One would be to have all three characters onstage. The other would be to have them come and go in accordance with their monologues. If we would be onstage the whole time, each of us would have one-third of a small space. If we came and went, set pieces would also have to come and go or, if they stayed throughout, again only part of a small set would be available for each of the actors to work in. So, under any circumstances, there would be no need for major blocking. There simply wouldn't be enough space to do any.

Nonetheless, the three characters are clearly defined in the script in terms of their space and in terms of their costuming. The differences would call for a specifically designed space for each character to play in. My space, clearly indicated by the script, would be in Martin's office lodged in a skyscraper high above downtown St. Louis. The setting automatically suggests certain things—a desk, a chair, perhaps some bookshelves still partially filled, and maybe a window, since Martin refers to the outside several times. One speech in particular begins with him looking out at the Mississippi River. Martin must also be well dressed. He makes many direct references to his clothing and to the attire of others. I would have to be dressed in appropriate lawyer threads, top of the line. I would need to wear a suit and tie, because the script refers to this fact. But since my section of the play takes place late into a Sunday night–Monday morning, perhaps the jacket would be off by this point, or perhaps there would be an appropriate place in the script for me to take it off. Already I was thinking of physical actions to amplify what my character might be thinking and feeling.

The logical deductions I had made based on my script analysis gave me a framework to use as I would rehearse myself on my feet. Since blocking consists of movement from place to place, gestures appropriate to my character, and any ongoing business that my character might engage in, I already had an arsenal of basic ideas to work from. As I built my character physically, I would work from the fact that I had on a suit and tie with an expensive shirt with French cuffs always down (a reference directly from the script). I could get a lot of mileage out of that. I imagined I had a desk with all the things that might be on it, that I had a chair that would give me positioning possibilities and could make me look and feel powerful, plus I would be packing as an ongoing activity. There was also a window and a bookshelf to go to and from, as well as all sides of the desk to circumnavigate or lean against. My playing field and uniform were now defined and ready to use.

Without going into a lot of detail, I built my physical story organically. If, for instance, the script referred to a letter, I would go to the letter and find a way to use it for emphasis. If it referred to clothing, I modeled mine to emphasize the point, making sure that what I did not only fulfilled my objective, but that the manner in which I did so showed something about myself, as well. I got a lot of mileage out of looking at pictures of my family. This action is referenced specifically in the script, but I was able to show how I felt about my wife, my son, and my daughter whenever I handled their framed pictures and looked at them. I could show love, anger, and/or disappointment simply by how I related to these items with my eyes and my hands.

Since I had determined that my character was notably self-assured and egotistical, I asked myself what gestures would demonstrate those qualities, and when I found myself gesturing organically, I modified my natural movement in accordance with what I knew about Martin. I also began to make a study of powerful and egotistical people in my life and on television—politicians, for instance—and stole some of what they did physically for my character. I modified the way I stood, the way I walked, the way I got up and sat down, using my imagination, or what I had picked up from observation, or both. Molding and melding how I did an action with the "when and where" I chose to do so helped me tell the story of the play even as it helped me reveal my character.

I also looked for and found ways of using my physical space that would amplify what was going on in the story and with my character. In my fifth speech, for example, the playwright provided a mood change. My character went from bombastic to reflective. The speech started with Martin commenting on how he likes to watch the Mississippi River late at night and what the river has meant to him. I began the section by being drawn to the river view through the window. I slowly got up; moved to the window, still glued to what I saw beyond it; and eventually leaned against the wall—my focus still riveted to the view in the distance. This reflective sequence of actions set a tone for the scene and strongly affected my manner of word delivery. It gave me a starting point in the speech that would arc beautifully into a very powerful ending several minutes later. But the mood and the work grew out of my physical choices. In a later scene I pounded the arm of my chair in a way that reflected the manner in which the police had pounded my door in the middle of the night. The noise of the action shocked the audience and energized me in a way that helped me feel the emotional circumstances that fueled my character at that moment of the play.

By the end of my prerehearsal self-rehearsing, I could check off the following items:

- I understood the script.
- I had made choices intended to serve the play and reveal my character.
- I could say the words and deliver the actions in a manner intended to make my part in the play clear and exciting.
- I had attempted to serve the play, my character, and the playwright in all my efforts.

The question remained as to whether my director would agree with my assessment and choices, and whether it would all ultimately work for the audience, even if he did.

There could be no question, however, as to whether I would begin my return to the stage prepared to do so. In spite of still being scared to death at the prospect, I knew I was prepared and ready, come what may, to hit the beach.

In summary, then, here in list form is the game plan I use for preparing a role. The process has served me well.

Determine what the story is specifically

Map the throughline or story arc

Find moments of victory and defeat, moments of discovery, and any other moments that might cause my character a change in direction, emotion, or intent

Find ways to tell the story effectively, including:

- understanding how the playwright has laid out his story
- finding ways of providing the physical enactment of this story through what you do, physically and verbally
- determining the conflict and finding your objectives.
- defining each moment specifically through how you say and color the lines, how you fill them emotionally, and the physical actions ultimately selected and executed
- studying the music of the lines as written, paying attention to built-in tempos, rhythms, and vocabulary specific to your character
- using operative words
- shaping your work to ensure there are beginnings, middles, and ends with and appropriate dramatic builds
- making necessary in-the moment adjustments by listening and reacting

Of course, you will need to develop your own approach to working on a play. What I have listed here may or may not meet your needs precisely. That is perfectly all right. Each actor is different. If something works for you, you will want to keep it in your arsenal. If it does not work for you, find and keep what does. It is your long-term job to learn as much as you can and keep what is most effective for you. But what you want is a system. A step-by-step approach that will not let you down, even in the most difficult acting situation. Once you have such a system, the time you spend acting solo will never be time wasted.

CHAPTER TWELVE

LEARNING TO VIEW DRAMA AND THEATRE CRITICALLY

BEING ABLE TO ANALYZE AND CRITICALLY RESPOND TO the work of other actors in a classroom or studio setting is a necessary part of your artistic exploration and craft development. It will help you develop the ability to look for what is important in the work and how to apply it to your own efforts. It will also help you learn to focus on what will make you look good as an actor and serve your storytelling obligations.

Unfortunately, I have noticed in recent years that beginning actors have become increasingly less able to tell the difference between what is good or bad theatrically, and why something works or not. This is particularly true of their perception of stage acting, though not exclusive to it. Surprisingly, many students, even in a rigorous BFA program like the one in which I teach, have seldom if ever seen a professional production of a play, if we exclude musicals. And, though they may be familiar with television and movie acting, they have never really been asked to make analytical judgments of what they have seen, and in many cases they have never separated what they like from what is good.

But the problem, certainly in recent years, goes much further. It's not only that students have not seen much in the way of drama. They have read very little of it, as well. Many of the students who come into my program, for example, are set on becoming actors, yet the majority of them have read very few plays, and their analysis of them was, for the most part, from a literary angle (usually in English class) rather than a dramatic one—if there was any kind of analysis at all.

If asked, many of my freshmen probably couldn't tell you anything about the work of Sophocles, O'Neill, or Albee. And names like Pinter, Mamet, or Shepard might not even be familiar. The question then becomes, how can students begin their acting training when they are not even familiar with the material they are going to be dealing with? Does this sound like you, by the way?

If this description fits you, then please realize that your journey toward mastery will be much more difficult because you have begun your travels without a frame of reference. If you don't understand how drama works, how can you expect to create effective, artistic work? If you have no standard by which to judge what is good, then how can you accurately gauge your own product or progress? How can you become a better actor if you have no sense of what quality is? If you don't address these issues now, you will be like the blind man who must draw that proverbial elephant he has never seen. Examined in this light, it is not so strange that my freshmen tell me that a movie like *Saw 3* is a winner. Or when I send my students off to see *Mystic River* or *Crazy Heart* for the acting work, they return to tell me it was too slow and boring.

This display of questionable critical judgment, along with the fact that some of my beginning students have no background in the source material of their chosen field, concerns me greatly. It is the reason I begin my students' acting training with an intensive unit on understanding theatre—from the basic elements laid out by Aristotle, to a study of how theatre works. We also examine certain plays in class after they have been read independently, and we connect the reading to some basic concepts that you will find listed here. It is impossible, of course, in the limited amount of time we have together, to ever spend enough in-class time reading and discussing plays as a group. So, in addition, I have also begun to ask my students to read plays outside of class and to write short summaries and evaluations—much like you may have done as students in middle school. My actors, for example, must read a certain number of plays during the semester to meet the obligations of the course. By doing so, they are, hopefully, beginning to formulate some concepts about the variety of drama out there, and they are beginning to examine more closely how drama works onstage. This is something you might want to begin doing, as well. If you are serious about your acting career, you shouldn't need the threat of a bad grade to get you on board with this idea.

Remember, the actor's job is inextricably connected to the overall purpose of theatre, and an actor's purpose—to tell the story compellingly and clearly—is certainly part of theatre's overall mechanics. In the early sessions of their training, I introduce my students to the following concepts:

- How theatre holds a mirror up to nature
- That good theatre should be entertaining and enlightening in amounts dependent on the inherent qualities of a particular play
- That there are varying genres of plays, and that the mechanics of each and the necessary stylistic choices change in accordance with the requirements of the play
- That theatre is intended to be seen by an audience
- That the audience's perception is an important consideration in all artistic choices
- That an actor's internal and subjective feeling about the work may not be as important as how the work is perceived by an audience
- That a script is merely a blueprint for a staged production
- That playwrights write plays to be produced, not simply to be read
- That successful plays tell good stories that are based on conflict and are not simply warehouses for important ideas
- That those important ideas come out of the play as a result of story and character, not as their own entities

Early in their training, I also make my students memorize my definition of good acting—*acting that is believable and tells the best possible story while serving the script.* I tell them this is their compass, and no matter what the acting situation, if they connect what they are doing to this mantra, they will be able to make and execute choices that will work. So will you.

More and more over the years, I have come to believe that serving the script is something that, as a teacher of acting and of theatre in general, I need to spend more time on. And reading and seeing plays, as many of them as possible, is absolutely essential for developing students of acting. You must understand the variety of source material that is out there, and it is essential that you come to understand how the machinery of drama works. You can't assume that interpreting a script is something you will learn by osmosis, especially if you have little or no background in seeing plays, let alone reading them. The good choice, the one that serves the play as well as the character, is something that for most actors cannot be left to intuition. The choices you make, along with those of the director and the designers, affect whether the story of the play and its meaning come across clearly and effectively. Learning to recognize the story within a script and then being able to bring it to life is a critical part of your craft. Hopefully, you realize that by this point in the book.

But recognizing what works and what doesn't or what is good or not so good when you watch it is equally important. Not being able to do so would be not unlike asking a med-school student to read the anatomy books without ever having the chance to examine a body. Watching professional productions of plays and analyzing them critically can be like the dissection process for a med student. It will give you a chance to compare the dogma found in your reading and in your classroom work with the actual theatrical bodies—the good, the bad, and the corpses. By giving yourself your own dissections to perform, you will have a far more powerful tool than talking in the abstract.

What I propose is that you give yourself a series of plays to read, and then watch a production of each live or recorded. For practical reasons, you'll probably opt most often for a recorded version of a play, and sometimes you will have to settle for an adaptation of a play on film. A caveat, though. When a play is converted to film, invariably it is changed, often substantially, usually by adding characters and resetting many scenes to different locations. This kind of change has become a near absolute in film, because, unlike in theatre, a film can easily use multiple settings, and producers think that is what moviegoing audiences demand. More often than not, unfortunately, these changes weaken the original script—bad for the play and audience, perhaps, but not necessarily bad if you're training in critical analysis.

I suggest that you put your thoughts about a play you've read in writing. It forces you to be very clear about what you saw and heard in your head and what you think. Admittedly, you may not like the idea of having to write, but there can be little argument that making yourself think critically and putting it on paper is an effective way to get yourself to think logically, independently, and analytically about the work you come across and, ultimately, want to do. And there is little doubt that clarity of expression is often related to clarity of doing. Actors who can't relate clearly what they are trying to do verbally or in writing most often do not communicate it clearly in their work, either. If you select the right plays to read and the right recorded versions to compare them to, it will encourage solid critical thinking. That can only lead to better acting down the road.

Below you will find two listings of plays that can be read and used for discussion in the classroom. Included in the first list—a top-25, if you like—you will find brief entries that give you hints as to what to think about. The topics are related to those essential theatrical concepts listed earlier in this chapter. All of these titles have been tested in my own classroom. The second list includes many other great plays that represent the gamut of genre and style available out there. All these plays are all worthy of watching, and with the proper attitude, even the worst productions can offer a treasury of things to learn from.

Keep in mind that the titles listed here represent only a percentage of the plays you can actually find on tape or DVD. With some relatively easy sleuthing online, you will be able to get your hands on even the most difficult to obtain. But even if you don't have the time and energy to go on the hunt, there is still a host of plays or adaptations readily available for rent or purchase, particularly if you are a member of Netflix or head for Amazon.com. I believe that exposure to a wide variety of dramatic material can only serve to help you develop your understanding of what theatre is and how it works. Please note that the lists do not necessarily represent the plays that I feel are most worth reading; they simply represent a portion of the plays that I know to be available.

Agnes of God—John Pielmeier

The script offers strong, clear conflicts and characters who are revealed through playing out those conflicts. The basic dramatic elements are held together through a central spine clearly running through the play. Expectations raised in reading may be contrasted with what is produced in the film version. Is it a case of theatre versus Hollywood?

Amadeus—Peter Shaffer

A brilliant play with magnificent dialogue, turned into a very different film that is cinematic and equally brilliant. The difference between a play and a film could not be better presented—and both, miraculously, are by the same author.

Angels in America: Millennium Approaches—Tony Kushner

What is realism? And what happens when you mix genre and style—brilliantly? Heady social ideas come through plot and characters made theatrically and intellectually. How film can keep the virtues of a play, yet do what it can and must for a different medium, is well presented in this recent HBO movie.

Cat on a Hot Tin Roof—Tennessee Williams

A great character-driven play in which the conflict between characters allows those characters to reveal themselves. Lots of talk doesn't mean there is no action here. These are wonderful characters to dissect through what they say, how they say it, and what they do. Available recordings can demonstrate a lot about casting and production choices.

Crimes of the Heart—Beth Henley

A funny, quirky character play in which the humor is generated more through character behavior than punch lines. A reader can easily miss that Henley wrote a comedy. The movie version makes the same mistake. This film points up the difficult road that leads from page to stage.

The Crucible—Arthur Miller

Is the dialogue stodgy, or period? How do you act Salem, seventeenth century? Is this realism, or are the characters archetypal and larger than life? Does it work on the page? Does it work on the stage? How do you make the play's themes come through without being didactic? What does the film version do to the play? How does it stack up?

Dancing at Lughnasa—Brian Friel

A beautifully written, moving play on the page. Character and language exceptionally written. Does the film, in spite of a wonderful cast, fail to rise to the occasion? If so, why?

Death of a Salesman—Arthur Miller

A must-read for any American theatre student. Does it preach too much? Is it still relevant? Is the plot and dialogue too clunky? Why or why not? Several versions available to explore the variations on Willie-ness. Which interpretations work best and why? What is the relation between character interpretation and how the play is perceived?

The Grapes of Wrath—John Steinbeck

How do you put a journey on a stage and make it work? How do you handle a large cast and use them even when they're not the ones speaking? See the difference between using theatrical convention and style instead of film's literalism. Ideal for learning about the difference between the script and performance, between the stage and film. Use more than one version. The pictures are worth a thousand …

Hamlet—William Shakespeare

The play is vast, and no director's vision can embrace it all. Several fine film versions and a Kevin Kline version recorded from the stage demonstrate that a theatre production is a result of thousands of interpretive choices.

Hedda Gabler—Henrik Ibsen

First great modern female protagonist, or is she an antagonist? Iconoclastic in its time, now seems fairly familiar. How do you make Hedda work for a modern audience? Interpretations vary greatly, and at least three good ones are available on tape and DVD.

The House of Blue Leaves—John Guare

Wonderful comic characters who speak directly to the audience and deliver fabulous monologues. What genre of play is this, anyway? Sometimes it seems farcical, other times tragical. What is the unifying style here, and how do you make it work? The Lincoln Center production may provide the answer.

The Importance of Being Earnest—Oscar Wilde

Where dialogue is king. Fail to make the language fly and you've got a turkey. Is it farcical and broad, or realistic? Depends on whether it's the high school production, or the Royal Shakespeare Company, which can sell the Wilde wit effectively. Gotta make it work—any way you can.

"Master Harold" … and the Boys—Athol Fugard

A beautiful, beautiful play in all respects—characterization, language, spine—with a taped production to match. Well worth the time spent on this play. Harold is in some ways a villain, but the play works best when we care about him. How do the playwright, the actor, and the production make that happen?

Medea—Euripides

Conflict, action, unity of time and place. The basic Aristotelian elements of drama ready to be discussed. How does the play work best for a contemporary audience with contemporary values? Various versions with great actresses using various acting styles and choices. Which add up to the most affecting production?

A Moon for the Misbegotten—Eugene O'Neill

Too many words, but this play manages to move us because its characters touch us deeply. How does O'Neill make that happen? The production with Jason Robards and Colleen Dewhurst makes us forget that there are too many words, because the actors are busy making moment after lovely moment. How do they do that?

'night, Mother—Marsha Norman

The conflict doesn't get more basic than this. Life-and-death time on stage and only two characters to make the action soar. A basic study on the machinery of drama based on strong conflict. The film version manages to compromise a perfect piece of machinery. Worth watching for how it manages to do that.

Noises Off—Michael Frayn

One of the most brilliant examples of farce ever written. Dialogue clearly takes second place to action—mostly of the physical kind. A great way to demonstrate that acting is far more than being about dialogue. Since this play includes a play within a play, the importance of an audience is demonstrated in the film version by its lack thereof.

Oleanna—David Mamet

The best plays don't preach, they show. They lay out the pros and cons and let the audience draw their own conclusions. If this play is balanced as a script, a production must tread carefully to keep that balance. Read the play and watch Mamet's own direction of his material on film. Is it balanced? Why doesn't it work? Or does it?

Our Town—Thornton Wilder

American classic; simple, solid storytelling, where characters reveal themselves through action and dialogue, and the play's spine gently reveals itself as the play unfolds. Several versions to compare choice in action.

The Piano Lesson—August Wilson

A beautifully written play that is literary as well as theatrical. Filled with language and symbol, and yet the engine is in the strong conflict and clear characterization. The filmed version falls short of the play as written, in spite of fine performances. Why?

A Streetcar Named Desire—Tennessee Williams

Is this the *great* American play? Room for debate, but there is no doubting its place in the culture, and so—a must-read. Great language, character, and dialogue, and its combination of theatricality mixed with a seeming realism makes for great discussion. Comparing the Brando version with any other makes for a great illustration of how choices and casting affect a production.

True West—Sam Shepard

Conflict taken to the limit, and yet the play is hilarious—though your students may miss this fact on a first read. There's Shepard's heightened poetic language, and two central characters that form a fabulous comic act. The recorded version with Malkovich and Sinise is nothing less than brilliant. Careful, though, this one may be far beyond PG.

A Walk in the Woods—Lee Blessing

A simple two-character play in which conflict reveals character and theme with a lovely simplicity and effectiveness. The production serves the script even while the acting work deepens it. Worth looking for.

The Women—Claire Booth Luce

Lots of witty and dated dialogue spoken by characters from a world long gone. May be too much verbiage to hold a contemporary high school student when reading from the page. But the vintage film version compared to the recent production shown on PBS can help students see the difference from page to stage. Finding the right style, a must for this one.

Other plays available on Tape or DVD:

Ah, Wilderness! Eugene O'Neill

All My Sons Arthur Miller

Antigone Sophocles

Antigone Jean Anouilh

Awake and Sing! Clifford Odets

Barefoot in the Park Neil Simon

Betrayal Harold Pinter

The Boys Next Door Tom Griffin

Brighton Beach Memoirs Neil Simon

Bus Stop William Inge

The Children's Hour Lillian Hellman

For Colored Girls Who Have Considered Suicide … Ntozake Shange

Curse of the Starving Class Sam Shepard

Cyrano de Bergerac Edmond Rostand

A Delicate Balance Edward Albee

Dinner with Friends Donald Margulies

A Doll's House Henrik Ibsen

Endgame Samuel Beckett

Equus Peter Shaffer

Fifth of July Lanford Wilson

Fool for Love Sam Shepard

The Front Page – Ben Hecht and Charles MacArthur

Getting Out Marsha Norman

Glengarry Glen Ross David Mamet

The Heidi Chronicles Wendy Wasserstein

The Homecoming Harold Pinter

Inherit the Wind Jerome Lawrence and Robert E. Lee

Julius Caesar William Shakespeare

The Laramie Project Moisés Kaufman

Love! Valor! Compassion! Terrence McNally

M. Butterfly David Henry Hwang

Macbeth William Shakespeare

Major Barbara George Bernard Shaw

The Man Who Came to Dinner George S. Kaufman and Moss Hart

Marat/Sade Peter Weiss

Marvin's Room Scott McPherson

Of Mice and Men John Steinbeck

A Midsummer Night's Dream William Shakespeare

The Miracle Worker William Gibson

Miss Julie August Strindberg

Much Ado about Nothing William Shakespeare

Oedipus Sophocles

Orphans Lyle Kessler

Othello William Shakespeare

Picnic William Inge

Prelude to a Kiss Craig Lucas

A Raisin in the Sun Lorraine Hansberry

Reckless Craig Lucas

The Rimers of Eldritch Lanford Wilson

Rhinoceros Eugène Ionesco

Romeo and Juliet William Shakespeare

Rosencrantz and Guildenstern Are Dead Tom Stoppard

The School for Scandal Richard Brinsley Sheridan

The Seagull Anton Chekhov

Steel Magnolias Robert Harling

She Stoops to Conquer Oliver Goldsmith

Six Characters in Search of an Author Luigi Pirandello

Six Degrees of Separation John Guare

The Skin of Our Teeth Thornton Wilder

Sleuth Anthony Shaffer

Streamers David Rabe

The Substance of Fire Jon Robin Baitz

SubUrbia Eric Bogosian

Talk Radio Eric Bogosian

The Taming of the Shrew Shakespeare

Tartuffe Molière

The Time of Your Life William Saroyan

Three Sisters Anton Chekhov

Twelfth Night William Shakespeare

Uncle Vanya Anton Chekhov

Uncommon Women Wendy Wasserstein

Waiting for Godot Samuel Beckett

Who's Afraid of Virginia Woolf? Edward Albee

Wit Margaret Edson

The Zoo Story Edward Albee

Zoot Suit Luis Valdez

Keep in mind that no matter how effective any of the taped or DVD versions listed may be, there is still nothing to equal actually getting to as many live theatrical productions as possible—if they are professional productions, all the better. There is so much to be learned about focus, about ensemble, about collaboration, and about the relationship between audience and performers that is impossible to experience from watching a TV screen, in spite of the excellence of any particular production. On the other hand, reading and then seeing productions of plays—even recorded or filmed ones—is absolutely essential. The once-removed experience of watching a recorded theatre or film adaptation is far better than not having had the experience at all.

Whatever your critical opinion turns out to be on any particular play, make sure that you have thought through that opinion clearly and carefully. Be sure you can support what you think with specifics drawn from the production. Your opinion is always valid, but only if you can make a case for what you think. There is always room for a great variety of reactions, particularly when you are dealing with issues that are subjective—issues like what is good or bad. But never let yourself get away with an unsupported opinion. Finding your reasons for thinking and feeling as you do will help you grow. Be sure to think about a production's success or failure in terms of its mechanics. What were the choices? Did they work, did they fail to work, and most importantly, why? You might want to compare your opinions to those that critics had. It's easy to do that nowadays. Just get online and find a raft of critical responses from newspapers, websites, et cetera. See how others think, and compare what you read to your own responses. There's no way you can't learn from this process.

In the end, you should be discovering and developing your understanding of the machinery of drama. A play's clarity of meaning, and its ability to move us intellectually and emotionally, is invariably tied in to its ability to adhere to basic structural rules. Making choices counter to these rules is unlikely to produce successful results. By learning to recognize, examine, and understand these rules, whether in script form or in production, you will be helping yourself to succeed. When it comes time to make your own choices, you will be making them in such a way that they best serve the intentions of the playwright, the story being told, and the obligations of the production. And when these obligations are being met, you will also be serving yourself as an actor and as an artist.

CHAPTER THIRTEEN

MASTERING YOUR CRAFT

AS I AM WRITING THE FIRST DRAFT OF THIS CHAPTER, another school year is drawing to a close. If your time goes anything like mine, once again you're breathless and amazed that another year has gone by so fast. It's a take-stock time for me, because in a few days I will be called upon to evaluate—artistically as well as academically—the students I teach and, in some cases, to decide whether they will be invited back into the program for another year of professional training. This is always a difficult time for me, because I have to make judgments about the talent my students possess and whether I think they have a chance to make it in the business they are training for. This is a godlike responsibility, and one that I am not comfortable carrying. Who am I to judge this subjective quality, and what crystal ball do I have that allows me to peer into the future to determine who will have the stuff success is built on? How can I determine which of my students will develop the craft or have the luck or the personality to succeed? Bottom line, I don't. But acting is a difficult career choice at best, and it is necessary that I give the evaluative process my best shot, since my program requires that I do so.

Unlike some other BFA programs, ours has no quotas. It is our intention that if eighteen students enter our acting programs, eighteen will graduate with BFA degrees four years later. This is never the case for various reasons, but nevertheless, it is our hope. Since I cannot judge potential for success, except through subjective means, I have come to rely heavily on a student's commitment to the development of craft. How hard a student works and the growth a student demonstrates in craft are for me every bit as important as the talent that student demonstrated at his or her entry audition or continues to show each time he or she works. Talent is a given. It is a result of luck, genetics, or a gift that the gods have bestowed. It cannot be increased or diminished; it does not grow with good husbandry, nor does it go away with lack of application. But the craft each of us is offered can and must be learned, and it is up to each of us to develop this craft toward mastery.

So here I am at the time of year when I have to take stock of my students, and in no small way my opinion about each of them may affect their dreams for the future. If I give them the nod, I am stamping their passport to another year of training for a career in a very difficult field. If I refuse the stamp, I am throwing an additional obstacle into a career path that is already riddled with potholes, or worse, dashing to pieces the fragile dream they are dearly holding. Since from my students' point of view the stakes are so high, I wear my responsibility heavily and rely on how each of them has personally handled the mastery of their craft in the year they have just completed.

You may have spent the past year developing your craft through the rehearsal process of the plays you have been cast in, or through your performance experience, or by attending acting classes in your school program, or through a combination of these things. So, if you'll permit me, I'd like to ask you a few big self-evaluative questions before you close the pages of this book.

How hard have you worked this past year to develop yourself as an artist? Did you work as hard as you could have? Or did you rely on your natural talents to get you by? If your answer was the "got by on natural talent" one, think about the fact that you have denied yourself a very important artistic opportunity this year and you may be on your way to developing a habit that will not well serve you as an artist, should you choose to continue your pursuits in theatre or film. Before you begin your self-analysis, however, let me offer you a few anecdotes that may help you better make some judgments about the way you have worked this year to improve your ability as an artist.

At the end of their sophomore year, I give my scene-study students a final in which they must put together a two-minute scene and mount it for presentation. They have about a week to ten days to put their final together. I offer them a half hour of my time for each scene at the beginning of their preparation week. During this session they do a first read of the scene and I give them feedback. That means that they have already read the play and analyzed it by the time I listen to the reading. They have also analyzed the scene for presentation and made the basic choices regarding conflict, objectives, given circumstances, beats, dramatic moments, and so forth—all the things you've read about in this book. This meeting constitutes the only input I give my students during the process. Several days later they put up the scene as their final presentation, with blocking, business, costumes, and anything else they choose to include. Most of the scenes I see are excellent. The work is clear, exciting, and specific. The actors are playing off each other because they are listening, and each moment is full and shaped.

"How is this possible?" is what I said to myself the first time I witnessed this phenomenon several years ago. Generally in my class, we spend three weeks to a month on each five-minute scene we work on, from first read to last presentation. The first reads usually miss the boat because of analysis and interpretation problems and because my actors are usually not listening to each other. The scene's first time on its feet is invariably problematic because the blocking is not well thought out and does not help make it clear and compelling. The blocking is usually inconsistent with the objectives of the characters and the structure of the scene as written. The next presentation often ignores the dramatic arc that must be created and maintained, and it skips over many of the important moments. In short, during their soup-to-nuts process, my students seem to need a lot of coaching and redirection to make their work first-rate.

But the finals my students put up seem to betray this pattern completely. With hardly any preparation time at all, they demonstrate they are actors who possess enough craft to analyze efficiently and economically and can transfer that analysis into actions that result in excellent work, and all this practically on their own. On one hand, I am thrilled to see the ability they obviously possess. On the other hand, I am disturbed because the entire exercise demonstrates that with proper work habits and more commitment and time, they would be able to accomplish far more work, and work that is far better. And let's face it, the more you work, the better you get. At the end of their sophomore year, my students invariably lament that they have done only six or so scenes. They realize how much they have learned during the course of the year and mourn the fact that they didn't work harder and faster—so they could have learned even more. Many admit that they could have done just that. "Imagine how much we would have learned if we had pushed ourselves," someone invariably offers—as though it is part of a year-end script memorized and delivered for the occasion.

A good way to turn that negative into a positive is to look at every acting opportunity—rehearsal, exercise, class, or performance—as a chance to work on craft, as a chance to do your art form, as a chance to grow as an artist. If you are still a student, your opportunity for growth is the most fertile it will ever be. You have the freedom to pursue your chosen work—the work you love to do. You actually have the job, and you didn't even have to audition. You can pursue the development of your craft unimpeded by the demands of making a living, raising a family, or the other commitments of adulthood that make finding time for your art so difficult. So commit to the pleasure of the task, and relish in it. If you squander the opportunity now, you will regret it later. The time you can spend now on mastery is a gift.

But keep in mind that working toward mastery is not just something students engage in. Throughout a career, the professional artist continues to doggedly pursue mastery, as well—because the true artist is compelled to seek new challenges, and there is always room to grow. If you are already working in the profession, you know this is true. For you, mastery may remain elusive and still just slightly out of reach. It may always be so. How, then, can an artist ever be truly satisfied? In fact, satisfaction is probably not possible. But this is really not a bad thing. Satisfaction can lead to stagnation, whereby an artist can doom herself to repeat what she has already done over and over again.

If you think of mastery as the top of the mountain you will never reach, but each successful step upward inches you toward your goal, you will continue to grow as an artist and find enormous satisfaction in the progress you are making. It is the journey rather than the ending that makes the story interesting. Stagnation is impossible if you use the metaphor being offered. Think in these terms and your own ascent toward mastery will be satisfying, thrilling, and rewarding.

Here's an example of what I mean. Some time ago we in our program had the pleasure of a visit from Douglas Sills, the star of Broadway's long-running hit *The Scarlet Pimpernel.* This production made theatre history, you may recall, because it actually opened to negative reviews but kept afloat during its early days based on good word of mouth, mostly a result of the star-making performance by Sills in the title role. Later, while running at night, the show was revamped and rerehearsed by day. It actually reopened (without ever closing) with a much-improved book and production and managed, this time with solid reviews, to run for an impressive length of time.

When you see Douglas Sills in person, particularly offstage, you instantly realize the meaning of the term *matinee idol.* Sills is incredibly handsome, stands well over six feet tall, and has flashing eyes that expressively sharpen or soften in accordance with the moment. When he enters a room, heads truly turn. Although he became famous in musical theatre, Sills was trained in classical acting at American Conservatory Theater in San Francisco, one of America's finest repertory companies and training programs. What really impressed me about him, however, was the fact that this guy really works hard at his craft. Here I was, looking at a guy who seems to have it all, a guy who probably has parts thrown at him, especially in musical theatre, where handsome, masculine men who can sing and act are at a premium. Yet, through remark after remark, Sills revealed himself as an artist who fits the description of the work ethic outlined in this chapter.

One story he told in particular struck all of us listening and has stayed with me since that time. It was so striking, in fact, that it is worth repeating here.

During some time off, Sills, who was already well known in the business for his showstopping work in *The Scarlet Pimpernel,* had an audition on the West Coast that was going to be held in a converted church. On the evening before the audition, Sills made a special trip to the church to check it out. He wanted to be familiar with the size of the room, its acoustics, and other pertinent information that could affect the performance of his audition—because he wanted his audition to go the best it possibly could. When Sills got there, he found that the building was locked and he would be unable to check out the space. Instead of giving up, he tried to find a security guard to let him in but could find no one. He did find an open window or door, however (I can't remember which), and let himself in. He actually rehearsed there for his audition the following day. I can't even remember whether he got the part he was trying out for, but the fact is that here is a guy who is interested in doing the best work he possibly can do and is willing to do what is necessary to make that happen. To put it another way, here is a performer who deserves the success he has achieved, because he is more interested in the quality of his work than in the trappings of success that so many performers mistakenly believe is the true validation. He is willing to work, and work hard, even though to others it may seem that he no longer has to.

Which brings up the issue of what success really means, and its relationship to mastery. Each year I read more than a hundred essays from aspiring applicants for our program. Most of the writers say they want to be stars and that our program's reputation for training will help them achieve that goal. Shockingly, only a few say in their essays that they want to learn how to act, so they can become the best performers they can be. I wince as I read—because training to become a star is not what training programs are about. Professional training programs are geared to develop your talents through craft, so that you can eventually find your way to becoming the best artist you can be. But fame and fortune are guaranteed to none and acquired by few. Training in the hopes that it will lead you to stardom suggests that, for most applicants, the training will be wasted. The fact is that only a small percentage of those who train in BFA programs actually become the brightest lights in the industry.

Therefore, in our pre-professional program, we spend a lot of time talking about the meaning of success. Our students are doomed to a life of unhappiness unless they replace the concept of success as stardom that they wrote about as incoming students with a better model. A far more reasonable and, frankly, more admirable standard of success—one more in line with the reality of an artist in today's world—is mastery. Mastery can be measured in personal growth rather than by money or fame, but more importantly, it is achievable. Unlike fame, that is as much a matter of luck as skill and may or may not have anything to do with craft or talent; mastery is dependent on the individual artist's ability to work hard, be self-disciplined, and possess a willingness to accept criticism and learn from it.

These are characteristics worth developing by you, as well, especially if you are pursuing a career in theatre beyond high school. In fact, you may want to begin your new approach now by ripping up that future college essay about wanting to be a star before it is written. Once it's in the trash, take a moment to picture yourself as that artist about to begin that climb up the mountain. The peak, which you can see with crystal clarity, is far away, but the challenge of the mountain awaits you, invites you, and compels you to begin your journey with optimistic spirit and determination.

So how about those questions I asked earlier on? Here they are again:

How hard have you worked this past year to develop yourself as an artist?

Did you work as hard as you could have? Or did you simply rely on your natural talents to get you by?

Only you know the real answers to these questions. Your teachers and your peers can only guess at whether you truly challenged yourself and whether you have given your studies the maximum effort you can. If you admit to yourself that you haven't, there is still plenty of time to change your ways. The mountain awaits you, and you will need to give it your very best effort. And remember, your success is in the journey itself.

Before you begin your climb, just a moment more, please. There are a few other questions—ten, to be exact—that you might want to consider. Take your time, and when you're ready, write down your answers, and your reasons for those answers. Be honest with yourself, because what you say is related to your potential for success later on. Learning to apply the most helpful answers to your own artistic development will ensure that your personal climb up the mountain will be a happy and successful one.

All right, then, here goes. Don't read beyond the questions until you have completed your responses.

1. Does the thought of failure keep you from trying?
2. Are you held back by the opinions of others?
3. Do you mistakenly feel that your work is not good if it is not perfect?
4. Does your idea of quality inhibit your ability to produce quantity?
5. Do you believe that art is something magical and therefore not producible by ordinary mortals?
6. Do you use having "no time" as an excuse for not working on your craft?
7. Do you get satisfaction from your work only when someone else praises you, or do you enjoy and get satisfaction from the process of working itself?
8. Do you spend a lot of time thinking about how your work stands in relation to your classmates'?

9. Do you believe that your future is in your hands, or are you willing to leave your future to fate?
10. Do you believe that you learn to do by doing?

Ready to discuss? Then here goes.

FEAR OF FAILURE IS UNHEALTHY TO AN ARTIST

The fact is unless you work, craft cannot be developed and art cannot be made. Every day in freshman acting, I ask for volunteers. Those who work get feedback. Those who get feedback have the opportunity to make adjustments and try again. They get to feel in their bodies the results of any adjustments made. These are the students who can then use their sense memories as well as their intellects to guide them through the next acting opportunity. Those who did not volunteer can read about mountain climbing, but, let's face it, that's a very distant second best to having the experience itself. Of course we can learn a lot from watching the work of others, but making the mistakes and getting the feedback is the fastest, most economical way of learning. If you're not getting up in class because you're afraid of the criticism, then you must get over this. Feedback and reworking is the core engine of growth.

THE OPINIONS OF OTHERS ARE NOT WHAT'S IMPORTANT

If the reason you're afraid of criticism is because it may be a reflection of what your peers and teachers think of you, get over it. The criticism of the work is not synonymous with their opinions of you, but even if it were, you must learn to get past this. If you are stymied or held back by what others may think, you're in the wrong business. Even Meryl Streep and Anthony Hopkins get their fair share of criticism, and often for work that I'd be mighty proud to have created. The truth is that acting, like all art, is in part a matter of opinion. And as the old cliché goes—everyone's got one. So as part of your training, you must learn to separate the useful parts of criticism from the parts that might otherwise hurt you or slow you down. Take what's useful and ignore the rest. The people who are surrounding you now will be playing no part of your life in just a few years, so why let their opinions hold you back or stop you?

LOOKING FOR PERFECTION IS UNREASONABLE

I have taught many students who wince as I give them notes on their work, or palpably shake their heads in an outward show of self-distain. As I offer the commentary on their work, I can see that their eyes are drifting off in response to some inner monologue in which they punish themselves for their failure to be perfect as artists. As a result they lose much of the objective part of what I am telling them. When they go off, they remember how it felt during my comments much better than they remember the comments themselves. When they rehearse the next time, they are unable to use what I have offered them—simply because it didn't register. If instead these students could learn to accept who they are and where they are in regard to their craft, they would function as developing artists far more efficiently. Keep in mind that separating art and craft is a recent phenomenon. It is very unlikely that early cave dwellers inhibited themselves from wall painting because they felt their work wasn't up to snuff. They left it up to us, several hundred thousand years later, to determine whether it was quality art or not. A good model. You do the work. The critics can determine later whether your work is worthy of being considered art.

QUANTITY COUNTS

My daughter is a gifted, brilliant, and wonderful girl who is seldom satisfied unless her work is perfect. She sometimes spends hours on projects and assignments that should take far less time. But she is committed to perfection and on occasion must be argued out of anything less. Sometimes she is unable to put her work into perspective and forgets that each of us has only a limited amount of time and energy to give to a single project. This characteristic gets in her way. It prevents her from accomplishing more of the things she might accomplish if she used her time more efficiently. In your classroom, with the limited time you have, you would be better off putting up less than perfect work—if it means getting to work more often and getting to apply the feedback that you receive. Your training is a process, and you need not be perfect in the studio. It is a place to learn from your mistakes, so relish in your mistakes and apply the corrections to the next step of the process. Work often and grow! You will scale the mountain more quickly if you do. Remember your job is to grow—leave the criticism to others. Perfection gets in your way; just learn the skills that can be learned through process.

IT AIN'T MAGIC, IT'S HARD WORK

When you have the opportunity to see art, it may strike you as magical. You can actually see the pulsating aura that surrounds it, and you are awed. If that makes you think trying to create art is something better left for those who possess this magic, think again. Read about almost any great artist, and you read of their trials and struggles to learn, make a living, and be recognized. Van Gogh, whose paintings now sell for $60 million, earned little or nothing from his artwork. People didn't like it. But that didn't stop him from working prolifically. When Isaac Stern played the violin, it may have sounded magical. But he practiced hours every day to the day he died—a man well into his eighties. Even Dustin Hoffman, who complained in *Tootsie* that an actor can't do his craft unless he's working, is well known to be an artist who labors tirelessly on his craft, even now, when his body of work has become the stuff of legend and he is considered an artist of the highest order. Invariably, the magic is a result of the work and craft behind it.

IF IT'S IMPORTANT, YOU MAKE THE TIME

No matter how tired you are, you almost always brush your teeth before you go to bed. You do so because you know this responsibility is important and you feel that you must keep your commitment. For many of us, this kind of commitment becomes so much a part of our lives that we barely need to think about it. Brushing has become a habit. When we learn to treat our artistic lives with the same kind of commitment, we will be able to make the time for it, and with enough practice this commitment will also become a habit. More importantly, once the habit is established, we will barely need to think about finding the time any longer.

My daughter is committed to mastering the piano. She plays almost every day. During the stretches of time when she keeps to a schedule, she has no problem finding the practice time. When she allows other things to interfere with her schedule, she sometimes fails to find the time, but the unspent practice time affects her and she finds a way to compensate in the next couple of days. As a result, her growing mastery of the piano is apparent to anyone who hears her play. I am well over fifty but look significantly younger because I stay in shape. In graduate school, some twenty-five years ago, my acting teacher told me that my body was my instrument. I have practiced four times a week since then. The results are apparent to anyone who sees me standing next to my old high school buddies. Bottom line—art gets done by doing the work. Learn to find the time.

LEARN TO GET THE SATISFACTION FROM THE WORK ITSELF

If you allow the satisfaction for the work you do to come from the praise of others, you have given away the control of your happiness. If you must wait for others to provide you with your happiness, you are likely to be at the mercy of others and may have to wait a long time. You are likely to spend very little time happy. Compete instead only with yourself. If you set your own goals, then you can be responsible for meeting them. By setting goals for yourself that you can reach, you will know how to make yourself happy and are likely to do so. You have given yourself the power and are providing yourself with built-in positive reinforcement for continuing to find the time to pursue your craft. The trick, however, is in accepting who you are and what you can do. No matter how much I exercise, I will never again be able to play Brick in *Cat on a Hot Tin Roof.* I'm just plain too old. But if I keep my goals realistic, I'll always find a way to please myself and get the satisfaction that will keep me going.

WORRYING ABOUT WHERE YOU STAND IS TIME AND ENERGY WASTED

Unfortunately, many of the students I teach judge their abilities and their future prospects by trying to figure out where they stand in the pecking order of their class, or by analyzing the way productions have been cast to determine who the most talented students are and how they stand in relation to those students. Maybe you do, too. This is a waste of time and energy. In the first place, no matter how prestigious the program, the university (or your high school) is a small pond when compared to trying to make it in the profession. New York is an ocean, and your school is a puddle in a rain shower. Why get all bent out of shape? The professional realities and competition you will face later simply don't make for a good comparison. Secondly, how one is cast in a particular production depends as much on who is needed in terms of type and who goes well with whom in a particular play as on how good you may be in an absolute sense. Thirdly, your learning curve may be such that where you stand as a sophomore in terms of development may change radically by the time you are a senior, and for some, the real jump in growth will happen later, after you graduate. So why go through all the torture of making comparisons? It's meaningless and will only bring you down or take energy and focus away from your commitment to learning, when that should be your only focus.

KEEP YOUR FUTURE IN YOUR HANDS

Do you plan on getting a job to pay your bills, or are you just going to buy a lottery ticket every week until your numbers come in? If you believe that your future success as an artist is predetermined or a matter of fate, you are relying on a lottery ticket to make your dreams come true. That means no matter how hard you work toward your goal, it doesn't matter, your future is ordained and will happen the way it is supposed to happen, no matter what you do. That works out fine if you're the lucky one. Are you really going to sit around and wait for your career to happen, like the guy with the lottery ticket? If you do, you are at the mercy of an outside force. Remember, only 20 percent of those who claim to be professional actors work.

Recently, a former student in our program returned to us to speak about his experience in show business. He has been very fortunate and has worked steadily since he moved to New York. Most of what he had to say was extremely helpful to our students, and we were glad to have him with us. However, he did say one very dangerous thing. Because he has been lucky in his career, he told our students, “I believe that if it is meant to happen, it will happen. I have seen good actors who work all the time, and bad actors that work all the time. I have seen good actors who never work, and bad actors that work all the time. There are no rules.” Even if what he said were true, what use is there in knowing it? If this is what you believe, then you have given away control of your life. Why bother working on your craft? Why bother pursuing your art? Your success is totally out of your hands. But if you choose instead to make mastery your goal, then whether you “make it” or not is not an issue to worry about and you remain totally in the driver’s seat of your chosen career. You can always pursue the mastery of your chosen art.

YOU ABSOLUTELY LEARN BEST BY DOING

No matter how many books on craft you read, no matter how many plays you read, no matter how many performances you see, it is still a far better learning tool to be doing the work. You learn from your mistakes and by attempting to fix them. You learn more by finding a new challenge to overcome and overcoming it; you learn best by setting a new goal and achieving it, over and over again. Make the work itself be your guide. Let it teach you your way of working. It will give you your discipline for doing the work, if you let it. It will teach you about your strengths and weakness and how to handle both. It will help you find the habits you need to keep doing the work throughout your life. So read the books, and continue to see the work of others—no doubt all this will help you grow. But never, never forget to keep doing the work yourself.

Finally, one more thought before you climb. The ones who become artists are the ones who do not quit. Art is about failing and starting again. Art is about achieving your reachable goal and finding another goal to replace the one you achieved—one that will take you farther up the mountain. Learn to accept that a career in the arts is one that constantly raises doubts, because growing into something new is untested—until you test it. Art is about mistakes, and surprises, and the certainty of uncertainty. Learn to accept all of this; better yet, learn to love it—because it is the life you will have chosen. Bon voyage! And keep working your craft, even if you're working solo. There's still plenty to work on.

GLOSSARY OF ACTING TERMS

This list of acting terms is not comprehensive. Many other terms representing other acting tools can provide you with further insights into the acting process and/or expand on what is presented here. Many terms not listed here are associated more specifically with an understanding of theatre overall but connect directly with the acting process. Still other terms relate to the playwright's craft, which you must come to understand in order to properly hone your analysis and choice-making skills. However, the terms and names listed in these pages can go a long way toward helping the beginning or developing actor get a picture of what must be done to strengthen his or her craft in an effective and economical way and with a necessary sense of artistic integrity.

ACTING

The most common definition I have seen goes something like this: "behaving believably under fictional circumstances." And that certainly describes the process. However, a more useful definition—one that I have come to employ over the years—might be the one that defines *good* acting. It goes something like this: acting that is believable and tells the best possible story while serving the script. All actors, of course, must be believable. The audience must accept an actor's work as he or she moves through the world of the play in a step-by-step sequence of action. *Believable* is not synonymous with *realistic,* however. A nonrealistic play may require choices that are not necessarily realistic but are consistent with the universe created by the playwright. The actor wants to tell the best possible story, as well—one that is the most interesting he or she can possibly create. That story, however, must be consistent with the intentions of the playwright and the production. Hugely entertaining choices by a character that are inconsistent with the overall needs of the play or production cannot be considered good acting choices. Each actor must make choices that contribute to the overall whole of the play and, like pieces of a jigsaw puzzle, must fit perfectly into the pieces that surround his or her character.

ACTION

This term has several meanings pertinent to the acting process. *Action* can refer to the cause-and-effect sequence of events in a play—essential for understanding the given plot and for making choices that are consistent with and supportive of that plot. This kind of action can also be referred to as the *throughline* or **arc.** The term *action* can also apply to any physical or psychological activity an actor carries out in the course of the play, as in "What is the action you are playing?" This kind of action is more frequently called an actor's **objective** or *intention.* It is important to keep in mind that no matter which definition of *action* is being employed, action is an essential ingredient of drama and closely related to the dramatic engine of all drama—**conflict.** Actors who focus on emotion or character, rather than on action, are in danger of falling into theatrical quicksand, for, as Stanislavski came to believe, actions are doable; playing emotion or character directly is less so.

ADLER, STELLA

A member of one of the most famous acting families in America and one of the original members of the Group Theatre, who challenged Lee Strasberg's interpretations of the Stanislavski system. She later went to Paris and studied with the Russian master herself. Upon her return, she explained Stanislavski's most recent theories of acting, which focused on physical action, to the Group Theatre. Lee Strasberg rejected these ideas and began referring to Stanislavski's earlier emotional work as "the Method," the technique Stanislavski later became universally famous for. Adler, too, went on to become one of America's foremost acting teachers, focusing on physical and psychological action, imagination, and the use of the script.

ANALYSIS AND SYNTHESIS

The intellectual tools necessary for breaking down a script and putting it back together so that it will work effectively for an audience. Good acting begins with an understanding of the play and the ability to make acting choices that serve that understanding. Contrary to the beliefs of some, acting is not simply about actors being able to personalize their feeling onto a script, but rather about communicating what characters think and feel to an audience so that the audience will understand the story of the play as written by the playwright—the story crafted by the combined choices of actors and directors to be as compelling and clear as possible.

ARC

Also known as the **action** or *throughline,* the *arc* refers the journey each character makes through the course of a scene or play, or to the sequential action of the play overall. It is essential that actors recognize and respond to each of the sequential events of the play and make **choices** that demonstrate how these events affect and alter them. The bigger the arc, the greater the journey, and the more the character changes during the course of the play. In general, the bigger the difference between the character at the end of the play and at the beginning, the more interesting the performance and the more interesting the play—provided the audience sees the actor making those changes as the character. It is up to the actors to understand the journey made by their characters and to communicate it through their chosen actions.

BEAT

The length of script during which an actor plays a particular **objective,** tactic, or **action.** A beat is always preceded by a transition and followed by another. The term, coined by Stanislavski, is actually result of a mispronunciation of the English word "bit" with a Russian accent, although there is a logic to the word "beat," as well. A particular beat (recognizable pattern or rhythm) is played until a victory, defeat, discovery, or new information causes the beat to end. When this occurs, there is a transition, at which point a new beat is established and played. As Stanislavski probably originally meant it, one bit (or small section of action) is followed by another and another, creating the throughline of the scene.

BEGINNINGS, MIDDLES, AND ENDS

The necessary steps that an actor must go through for all effective storytelling. Plays, scenes, beats, and even moments have beginnings, middles, and ends. So do all physical actions. Actors who fail to find the beginnings, middles, and ends to actions, moments, or any other aspects of their work will fail to be believable and will fail to execute choices that are clear and compelling for an audience. Most actions, for instance, start with the reason for the action. The actor who ignores this fact jumps into a middle and fails to communicate believably the story sequence he is undertaking. Dialogue, for instance, doesn't begin with the first word. It begins with the need to speak. Beginning actors doing a monologue often begin with the words rather than the need to speak. Because of this, it often takes them several moments before they connect with the words they are saying. The words have been wasted, and the actor looks bad. Here is another example. Try yawning. If you started with opening your mouth, you probably failed to execute a believable yawn. Yawns start with the impulse to yawn. So does an acting moment. The yawn is complete not when the physical action of yawning is complete, but when the result that the yawn produces in the yawner is apparent to the yawner and to the audience. Only when the beginnings, middles, and ends are fully executed is the storytelling potential realized.

BLOCKING

The physical elements of storytelling onstage—movement, **gestures,** and **business.** It is often expected by actors that the director will provide them with their blocking in rehearsals. But as Stanislavski came to believe, the physical choices made by actors are as much a part of the acting as delivering the lines is. The physical actions executed by actors can tell as much about their characters and about the story as any other acting tool at the performer's disposal. Actors who can act with their bodies as well as with their voices, with or without the director's input, are better actors for the ability. Physical action, as Stanislavski came to believe, can connect actors with their truthful emotional center. But even without that connection, actors who can communicate thought and emotion to an audience through what they physically do are the strongest ones.

BUSINESS

Any ongoing physical activity an actor carries out while pursuing or completing an acting **objective** onstage. Smoking and drinking are examples of stage business that can add to the actor's characterization and believability—by giving details of the character being played through the manner in which he smokes or drinks. Business is almost always secondary to the main **action** of the scene and **objective** of the actor. Like driving a car, business can be executed without direct focusing, unless, of course, the business requires focus for a particular moment—lighting the cigarette, for instance. The specifics of the particular business, however, can help shape a moment or inform an audience what a character is thinking or feeling. If I choose to drag on my cigarette after being told that my wife has left me, it gives the audience information. The good actor uses business in a specific way to help shape the performance.

CHARACTER

One of Aristotle's basic elements of drama needed in order to have a play. Other elements include dialogue, action, idea, spectacle, and music. We often hear actors talking about "being their characters," "inhabiting their characters," and so on. We also hear about creating biographies of characters' lives before and after the action of the play. All this can be dangerous, especially to a beginning actor. Inhabiting character and living out imaginary biographies can lead actors away from fulfilling their responsibilities to tell the story of the play by making acting choices for their characters that come from the script. Besides, becoming a character may be an illusion, or impossible for some actors to accomplish. Better to focus on the actions of each character and the manner in which those actions are performed. Character is **action,** and when action is combined with externals like costume and makeup, these actions go a long way toward becoming character.

CHOICES

Every actor must make choices about what her character needs from the other characters who surround her, and choices about the tactics to get those needs fulfilled. In real life people seldom think specifically about what they need, or, for that matter, about why they play out many of the actions they play out during the course of the day. Actors, however, must make choices for the characters they play, choices that get them closer to what their characters need, even if the characters themselves are unaware of why they do the things they do. This may sound simplistic, but the fact is when actors make choices that are seemingly too simple, choices that will get them toward their goal, they are making choices that invariably serve the built-in **conflict** of the plot. Any necessary complexity of character will be provided by the script and the audience's perception of character as they watch the action of the play. Positive choices are choices that help a character get what she needs. Negative choices are choices that do not do so. Actors should play only positive choices. Negative choices make for indulgent and often dull acting—because they diminish or destroy the potential conflict built into a scene by the playwright. Actors should not play their pain. They should acknowledge it and then make new choices that help their character get what she needs (i.e., that fulfills her objectives).

CONFLICT

When two opposing forces meet; the engine of all drama; the core ingredient an actor must recognize before choosing an objective. Playwrights want to tell the best story they possibly can. They know that the good story centers on a conflict—usually between a central character and the obstacles that character faces. Since that is the way plays are structured, actors must be able to recognize the conflict where it exists and make choices that contribute to that dramatic engine. When actors recognize the conflict in a scene and make their objectives relate to the other character who will be opposing the fulfillment of that objective, they are contributing to the conflict and to the dramatic success of the scene. Scene by scene, this approach almost guarantees an exciting, watchable story.

CRAFT

The tools of acting that can be learned and mastered, unlike talent, which is innate and cannot be learned. The mastery of craft can help the gifted actor hone and shape his work. For those less talented, it can go a long way toward substituting for the lack of natural gifts. Those who choose not to master craft will always have to gamble that their instincts are never wrong and constantly be at the mercy of those who seem to have control of the acting situation. Good directors, directors who are focused on and able to bring out the best in each actor, are hard to find. The actor who has mastered craft need rely only on himself to produce work that gets the job done.

CRITICISM

A necessary part of an actor's work. Without an outside eye to steer the course of an actor's work through critical observation and comment, the actor cannot improve the work she offers. Actors who see criticism as negative, or feel it as such, are actors who will have trouble enjoying the creative process and are likely to be difficult to work with. Criticism must be seen as a necessary and positive step toward making the final product the best it can be. Actors who cannot do this naturally must learn to do so quickly. It must be considered part of the craft.

DEFEATS

(See Moments.)

DISCOVERIES

(See Moments.)

EMOTIONAL MEMORY

The use of personal memory to create an emotion that can be used in an acting situation. This internal approach to acting was discovered and employed by Stanislavski in his early work and described in *An Actor Prepares.* He later abandoned this technique in favor of the external physical approach toward acting he wrote about in his later work. Method acting as described and taught by Lee Strasberg relied heavily on emotional memory—the application of real and honest emotions recalled from past experience and applied to the immediate acting situation.

EMOTIONAL TRUTH

The product of an actor who can find and produce honest emotions within himself that serve the acting situation he is engaged in. At one point Stanislavski felt that emotional truth was best found through the application of **emotional memory.** He later came to feel that emotional truth could better be found and repeated as a by-product of physical action that is more reliably repeatable and controllable. Today, most actors accept the validity of both approaches—some relying more heavily on one or the other, some using one or the other exclusively.

ENDOWMENT

Giving an object specific emotional meaning that can be effectively used for acting purposes. Every prop an actor uses has potential for creating wonderful acting moments—moments that can help communicate how the character is feeling or what she is thinking. When Dorothy picks up the ruby slipper, left by the late Wicked Witch of the East, for the first time, she does not simply pick it up. She endows the object with the emotion of the moment. When her three friends receive their worthless gifts from the Wizard, each endows the objects received with what those objects mean to them, thereby creating wonderful acting moments lasting only seconds onscreen but staying with the audience for the rest of their lives.

EXTERNAL AND INTERNAL

(See Emotional Truth and Physical Action.)

GENRE

The kind of play the author has written, such as drama, comedy, farce, tragedy. Each type of play has certain characteristics that must be acknowledged and adhered to and that may even require a particular style of acting if the play is to be acted effectively. A modern comedy, for instance, is expected to be funny, so the actor must make choices that support the playwright's intention. The actor must try to add to what the playwright has provided and certainly must never diminish what the playwright has offered up as the starting point.

GESTURE

A single specific physical action that communicates emotion, information, or attitude. A **choice** in a moment of the play to take one's hand and place it on the forehead after hearing that your daughter has died is a gesture. Shaking a fisted hand at an adversary after being embarrassed by him is also a gesture. Each communicates, through its simple execution, information and emotion about the character being played and about the thoughts and feelings of that character. Gestures can be a calculated, planned choice that through the rehearsal process become natural and organic, or they may be discovered spontaneously because they actually happen during the rehearsal process or in performance and, because they work, are adopted as part of the performance and used again and again by the actor at that particular moment of the play.

GIVEN CIRCUMSTANCES

The who, what, where, and when of a play or scene that must be considered before making acting **choices.** When a line from a play is delivered and makes sense in terms of the context of the play, an audience gives it little thought.

"Of course, that's the way it should be said," our subconscious would tell us, were we to ask its opinion. It is only when we ask a nonactor to say a particular line that he realizes that any line of dialogue could be said an infinite number of ways. Which is right? Which best serves the play? Which best serves the character saying it? Examining the given circumstances of the play, the scene, and the moment helps the actor narrow down the choices. The four W's refer to the *who,* the character saying the line; the *what,* the situation in which she finds herself; the *where,* the location in which this occurs; and the *when*, the time, both general and specific, of the occurrence. Take the line "I love you." How many ways can the line be said? Now narrow down the choices by manipulating the given circumstances. The number remains vast, but you are no longer operating in the dark.

HEAD-FIRST ACTING

A term coined by the author to suggest that good acting requires **analysis and synthesis** and that the best choices are ones that serve the story. More often than not, these choices must be thought out rather than simply intuited.

INDICATING

When a performer physically demonstrates an action without personal connection to what she is supposed to be thinking, feeling, or doing, thus "indicating" rather than fully committing to the action.

INTENTION

(See Objective.)

JOURNEY

(See Action and Arc.)

JUSTIFICATION

The process an actor goes through in order to make sure that a line or moment is acted in such a way that it is both believable and clear and that it makes sense in terms of the given circumstances of the situation. A line that is not justified will sound wrong or empty when delivered in the context of the play. It will sound like the actor is simply saying the line rather than having a need or purpose for saying it. Everything a playwright puts into a script is put there for a reason. An actor must discover those reasons and use these elements to support or enhance what is on the printed page or implied by it.

LISTENING

A basic requirement for an actor if she is to be believed, and an essential step for staying in the moment and reacting effectively. Actors who do not listen may be reliable performers, but their work never varies, seldom grows, and almost never presents the audience or their fellow actors the gift of spontaneity that being in the moment brings. Being able to adjust to the nuances of each fresh performance keeps an actor's work fresh and alive, and the magic found by simply being able to listen and respond to all that is happening in a freshly created moment is the ingredient that can make some actors' work so real and exciting. Those who simply wait their turn to say a line are easily distinguishable from good actors. So important is this skill that Sanford Meisner devoted most of his teaching time to developing this aspect of his students' craft. (See **Meisner, Sanford.**)

MAGIC IF, THE

An acting term coined by Stanislavski that reminds an actor to ask, "What would I do if I were this character in this situation?" Notice that the question is *do,* not *feel.* Because Stanislavski came to believe that playing out the appropriate actions told the audience more about the character's feelings and thoughts than did working with emotion directly, his "magic if" became an essential tool in his approach. Here is an example. Say you are Laura from

The Glass Menagerie. You have just been told by Tom, your brother, that your mother, Amanda, has died. What do you do? What do you feel? Act it now. You may be stuck, especially if you simply try to conjure up some emotional response. But what we know about Laura can give us some good starting clues to actions she might take, which in turn could provide the actor with a springboard for her emotional response. Perhaps Laura would go toward her menagerie to find some comfort. Perhaps she would pick up some pieces and examine them closely. Perhaps she would stroke her favorite or hold it tightly in her palm while putting it next to her cheek. Character and story can be communicated through what we do and how we do it. Asking "the magic if" can help lead us to those **choices.**

MEISNER, SANFORD

One of the great first generation of acting teachers that came from the Group Theatre. Meisner devoted much of his teaching time to finding techniques to better enable his students to listen well and stay in the moment. His most famous exercises are used by countless acting students around the world, whatever approach to acting they are studying. The Meisner repetition games, in which actors repeat what their acting partners say to them and try to turn these repetitions into actual conversations, have become a standard practice that is highly valued by all who teach and study acting.

METHOD, THE

An internal approach to acting centering on the use of emotional truth and sense memory; made famous by Lee Strasberg, but based primarily on early writings of Stanislavski. Critics of this approach, like Stella Adler, felt the Method was self-indulgent and often made actors look good at the expense of the play. Even she could not disagree, however, that the Method was a highly effective technique for film acting, where only a **moment** might be shot at a time, and the intimacy of the camera demanded an emotional presence and honesty not necessarily required by stage acting.

MOMENT

The smallest unit of dramatic action that can be acted. Actors must learn through effective analytical reading and good **listening** while in rehearsal and performance where moments occur and pick up on the execution of them. Every created moment is an important contribution to the overall story and to the story of each individual character. A fully realized moment has to be clear and full and most often has a **beginning, middle, and end.** Moments can occur at any justified time but most often are found at the end of a **beat** following the delivery of new information, when a discovery is made, or when there is a victory or a defeat in terms of the actor's objective. Any new information an actor as character learns should be reacted to. Examples from *The Glass Menagerie* include when Amanda learns that Tom is planning to leave, or when Laura learns that her mother knows she has not been attending business school. Examples of a discovery are when Olivia realizes why she has been given a ring from the Duke in *Twelfth Night,* or, from *As You Like It,* when Rosalind (disguised as a man) realizes that Phoebe is in love with her. Victories are the actable moments when objectives are reached. When Tom wins the argument about his leaving home and Amanda accepts the fact is a moment (although followed by a transition during which Amanda comes up with a new strategy and new plan of attack). Or when Jim convinces Laura to join him on the floor of the living room, thereby breaking through her wall of resistance, that is a moment of victory, as well. Those same moments are defeats for Amanda and Jim respectively, and the actors playing them have and should take the opportunity to respond in those moments. These kinds of moments are often followed by moments of transition—equally interesting and equally important to act. (See **Transitions.**)

MOMENT TO MOMENT

Refers to the ability of the good actor to respond to what an acting partner is saying and doing at a particular moment. Moment-to-moment acting requires good listening and is essential for believability, spontaneity, and the discovery of actions that can define a **moment.**

MOTIVATION

The reason behind a character pursuing a particular objective. Motivation cannot be played directly but can be used as a device to find the acting objective that can and must be played at every moment of a character's stage life. Here is an example. I am jealous of my brother. My mother always liked him better. How do I play jealous? I cannot. But I can try to hurt him whenever possible—to get back at him for taking all our mother's love. Jealousy is the motivation; punishing my brother is my objective. I can and should play my objective.

MOVEMENT

The aspect of **blocking** when an actor travels from one place to another onstage. There should never be purposeless movement by an actor. An actor crosses the stage because his character needs to put distance between himself and another character, or because he needs to cut down the distance between them. If an actor chooses to move away from someone or something, he is also moving toward someone or something else—with purpose. These movements have **beginnings, middles, and ends,** and the character should acknowledge these steps onstage to help him communicate his thoughts and feelings. Any movement should be connected to the actor's particular **objective** at any given time. Since physical positioning can help a character get what he needs or keep another character from getting what she needs, the physical relationship between characters onstage should be used to establish or maintain power and weakness that tie in to a character's objective. The good actor is aware of this and uses this tool to pursue his purpose and help reveal his inner life to the watching audience.

NEGATIVE CHOICES

(See Choices.)

NEW INFORMATION

(See Choices.)

OBJECTIVES

The needs an actor playing a character must pursue at all times onstage. Acting is not the same as life; it just closely resembles it when well done. No matter how well the actor probes the psyche and emotions of a character from the printed page, to some extent the actor is pretending. His words are not his own; they are borrowed from the playwright, who has written them for just this purpose. In life a person's actions are often random, and where they will lead, a person never fully knows until they are played out. Life is messy, often leaving many loose ends. A character in a play, on the other hand, is a creation resulting from the imagination of a playwright with the power to select and control the actions of that character—so that they play out in accordance with the action of the play being written. It follows, then, that a character's behavior is simpler by far than that of a living, breathing person. Each choice, each action the actor as character chooses and plays must therefore support the track the playwright has laid out. By pursuing the goal of the character, whether the character is aware of that goal or not, the actor creates the illusion of reality while making choices that ultimately serve the story of the character and of the play. Most objectives should be connected to the other characters who share a scene. Chances are that if a playwright put two characters in a scene, the **conflict** lies between those characters. The objective—to win something from that other character—most often arises from that conflict.

OBSTACLES

The elements in a scene or play that keep a character from obtaining his **objective.** They provide **conflict** and heighten the **stakes** of any acting situation. These obstacles can be in the form of another character (Tybalt for Romeo). They can be internal (the struggle in Friar Lawrence to decide whether he should perform the marriage rites for Romeo and Juliet). They can be external (the politics of Nazi Germany that infuses *The Diary of Anne Frank*). Or they can be inanimate (the weather in *The Grapes of Wrath*). Whatever the category, obstacles help keep the actions of a character and the overall story of a play interesting and exciting. Ask yourself what obstacles Laura in *The Glass Menagerie* faces—internally, from another character, and as a result of the given circumstances of the play. Now do the same for Tom, Amanda, and the "gentleman caller." Notice how these obstacles make both the characters and the story of heightened interest. The actor must look for these obstacles in the script and use them to make his journey through the story as exciting as possible.

PHYSICAL ACTION

The tangible and visible things a character does onstage. Try playing anger directly. Take a moment now, and try to conjure anger. Did you feel it? Would I recognize this feeling were I an audience watching? Now make a fist and slam it on a table as though you were angry. Did you fully commit to the action? If you did, you probably felt anger. The audience watching probably would have recognized your action as anger, as well. Now plan a sequence of actions that tells a story and that communicates what you are thinking and feeling. Make your physical planning specific, and rehearse each action carefully in sequence. When you have done so, you are acting in the manner that Stanislavski describes in his later work. This kind of approach to acting is clear, interesting, controllable, and repeatable. So is the good actor's work.

POSITIVE CHOICES

(See Choices.)

PSYCHOLOGICAL ACTION

(See Action.)

RISK

A basic tool for producing interesting acting; the more risk taken, the more interesting the actor in a situation. Another term for this concept is "the big choice." What makes you the more interesting actor—simply doing what is believable, or making the most interesting believable choice possible? The actor who takes risks and does so in a believable manner is the one who get jobs—because she is the one who produces the most watchable work. The acting **moments** best remembered are the ones where the actor surprises you, yet you recognize the rightness of the choice.

SENSE MEMORY

The use of personal memory relating to smell, sound, taste, touch, and sight to enhance the emotional power of an acting **moment** or situation. The actor who must smell the imaginary flower onstage will enhance his work by recalling specifically the beautiful fragrance of a flower actually smelled. Sense memories are among the strongest we possess. We can often remember the moment we actually heard a song for the first time, how the house we grew up in smelled at dinnertime, the taste of the first lobster we ever ate. An actor must make real for himself all that he does onstage and find ways to communicate those things to an audience. By leading himself to precise moments in such memories of sense, he can apply what he discovers to the current acting work being portrayed.

STAKES

What is at risk for the actor as character as she pursues her objective? These discovered *stakes* can help the actor make the acting situation as interesting as possible. As Amanda pressures Tom to bring home a suitor for Laura (*The Glass Menagerie*), what is at risk for her? As Laura comes out of her shell to meet the expectation and pressure of her gentleman caller, what does she risk? When Romeo climbs the orchard wall, or when Juliet agrees to meet her new lover at Friar Lawrence's cell, what is each risking? In all of these cases, the characters are willing to chance an enormous amount in order to get what they want. Awareness of what is at stake keeps the danger factor high for the actor and tells the audience quite a bit about the characters they are playing. Finding the stakes in the situations less obviously risky is a more difficult trick. But since plays tell stories filled with conflict, the playwright has stuffed them with huge risk potential. It is up to the actor to find the high stakes and use them to make the work as exciting as it can possibly be.

STANISLAVSKI, KONSTANTIN

The Russian theatre director, actor, and teacher responsible for most of the basic craft used in actor training.

STRASBERG, LEE

The most famous of the great seminal American acting teachers, Strasberg developed "the Method," employed by many of the great realistic film actors of the postwar era.

STYLE

Simply put, the world of the play. Actors must know the world of the play in which they are performing and make **choices** in thought and **action** that are consistent with the other actors in the play and world created by the playwright. *Realism,* for instance, though referred to as an acting style, really refers to the kind of world created by the playwright—a world that seems very much like the one we inhabit in our own contemporary lives. American plays of the 1930s, such as *Awake and Sing!,* were examples of realism in the time they were written. Today their language no longer represents what we consider realism. But they present a consistent world throughout. The actor must understand and find a way to act believably within that world.

SUBSTITUTION

A technique in which an actor substitutes a parallel personal memory from her own life for a similar one in the play she is working on to enhance her emotional connection to a **moment.** Often used by **Strasberg** in his **Method** approach to acting. Though developed by Stanislavski, he later abandoned its use. **Stella Adler** found substitution to be a ridiculously distracting approach to an acting problem, because it separated the actor from being in the moment of the play.

TACTICS

The specific strategies an actor as character uses while pursuing her objective. Some acting teachers break **objectives** down into smaller units when analyzing a script. These are usually referred to as *tactics.* For instance, your objective is to get your father to let you use the car tonight. He is against the idea. How many approaches can you come up with to get the car before your father finally gives in to you? Make a list of your strategies. Those are your tactics. You use them one at a time until you accomplish your objective and get your father to put the keys in your hand. In a scene, an actor as character often goes through the same process, whether planned or spontaneously. Each strategy is a tactic employed until there is a recognition that the tactic has succeeded or failed, at which time another and another is thought up and employed—until your objective is fulfilled or abandoned.

THROUGHLINE

(See Arc.)

TRANSITIONS

The actable **moments** when one objective is given up and replaced with another. These transitions occur as a result of objectives being lost, won, or abandoned because of **new information,** an interruption, or a discovery. Often the transitional moment provides the actor with a wonderful opportunity to show the audience what she is thinking or feeling. Sometimes, however, the rapid switch to a new tactic or objective without hesitation can be extremely interesting, as well, but only if the audience understands the jump. Here are some examples. You have been pressuring your father for the keys to his car. He gives them to you, and a victory moment is played, followed by the finding of a new objective—to get him to give you gas money. Your father threatens that if you say one thing more on the subject of car keys he will ground you for a month—a defeat. While you are sweet-talking your father, there is a phone call for you and you find out that Billy got his dad's car for the evening—new information that changes the situation. During your tactical advance on Dad, your mother enters with news that Aunt Joan has been in a car accident—an interruption and new information that changes the situation completely. While Dad is denying your advances, he is very funny and charming. You realize that you would rather stay home with the family than go out—a discovery that forces you into a transitional moment.

VICTORIES

(See Moments.)

A FINAL NOTE

All of the terms listed in this glossary suggest that acting choices must come from the script if they are to well serve you as an actor and the play. In too many acting books and acting classes, the analysis process is assumed to be part of a separate activity that does not need to be focused on in the acting class itself. Hopefully, this book has helped you realize that this kind of thinking is a mistake. More importantly, what you have read in these pages has given you solid ways to integrate the analysis part of your work into what you do as an actor on your own. This is a necessity if you are going to be able to produce reliable, compelling work quickly and efficiently.

You have learned that you should never leave it to your director or acting teacher to supply the correct or effective way of looking at a play, a scene, or a moment. Nor should you assume that others will provide the key to making choices that will work to tell the story. The responsibility is yours. Some directors will provide you with what you need; some won't or can't. Some acting teachers will direct you rather than teach you how to make choices for yourself. When an acting teacher provides you with an answer that works and makes you look good, they are not teaching you how to find such choices for yourself. When this is the case, you remain at the mercy of others to make you look good. When a play is left in the hands of directors who don't know what the playwright's story actually is or how to tell it, both you as an actor and the playwright are likely to end up looking bad. Sadly, this is too often the case. If you are going to become an efficient and compelling actor, you must be able to tell the story well and find it on your own. It is my hope that this book has helped speed you along that road. Michael Dorsey was right. An actor needs to work with others. But, as actors, we also have to be able to work it solo.